◤SCHOLASTIC Pocket United States Atlas

SCHOLASTIC 💡 REFERENCE

An imprint of

◤SCHOLASTIC

Produced by Miles Kelly Publishing Ltd
Bardfield Centre, Great Bardfield,
Essex, CM7 4SL, UK

Publishing Director: Anne Marshall
Managing Editor: Becky Miles
Editorial Assistant: Gemma Simmons

Art Director: Jo Brewer
Designer: Tom Slemmings
Picture Researcher: Laura Faulder
Cartography: H L Studios

Consultant: Clive Carpenter
Text: Philip Steele

Scholastic Reference Staff

Senior Editor: Mary Varilla Jones
Assistant Editor: Brenda Murray
Flag Consultant: Dr. Whitney Smith,
Flag Research Center

Creative Director: David Saylor
Art Director: Becky Terhune

Managing Editor: Karyn Browne
Production Editor: Susan Jeffers Casel

Manufacturing Vice President: Angela Biola
Manufacturing Manager: Jess White

Reprographics: Anthony Cambray, Mike Coupe, Stephan Davis, Ian Paulyn

ISBN 13: 978-0-439-85215-9
ISBN 10: 0-439-85215-3

10 9 8 7 6 5 4 3 2   07 08 09 10 11/0

Printed in the U.S.A.

First paperback printing, January 2007

Contents

How to Use this Atlas

Inside this pocket atlas you can explore the states of the U.S.A., and learn about the people who live there. In addition, there is an introductory section that describes how maps are made and used, and talks about the weather and times zones of the U.S.A. It also features political and physical maps of the country.

Understanding the maps

This simple key shows you the different features, labels, and symbols that have been included in the maps. These will help you to understand them.

	forest and grassland	⊕ *WAS*	national capital
	desert	Jacksoı	state/province capital
	mountainous region	Laramie •	town
▲ Kings Peak	mountain	White House ◆	place of special interest
White R.	river	*C A N A*	country border
Lake Okeechobeı	lake		state/province border

Abbreviations

MTS.	mountains	lb	pound
R.	range	kg	kilogram
ST.	Strait	km	kilometer
cm	centimeter	m	meter
ft	feet	mi	mile
ha	hectare	sq	square
in	inch	mph	miles per hour
l	liter	kph	kilometers per hour

Important words

Some difficult words are explained in detail in the glossary.

Captioned photos

On most spreads, you will find a photo of one of the states. The caption beneath each photo will explain where it is.

Discover more

Some amazing things you never knew about a state are contained in these fact boxes.

Search and find

If you want to find a city or an area on the map, use the grid references to locate its exact position on the map.

Political map

The identification map at the top left of the page shows the states and how they relate to the surrounding land area.

Main text

Each state is introduced with interesting information about its geography, history, climate, and the people who live in it, and what they do to make a living.

State listing

Every state is named at the top right of the page for an easy at-a-glance reference.

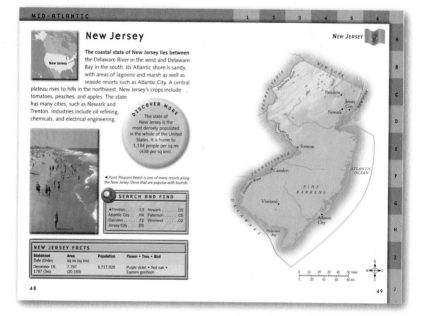

New Jersey

NEW JERSEY

The coastal state of New Jersey lies between the Delaware River in the west and Delaware Bay in the south. Its Atlantic shore is sandy, with areas of lagoons and marsh as well as seaside resorts such as Atlantic City. A central plateau rises to hills in the northwest. New Jersey's crops include tomatoes, peaches, and apples. The state has many cities, such as Newark and Trenton. Industries include oil refining, chemicals, and electrical engineering.

DISCOVER MORE
The state of New Jersey is the most densely populated in the whole of the United States. It is home to 1,134 people per sq mi (438 per sq km).

◀ Point Pleasant Beach is one of many resorts along the New Jersey Shore that are popular with tourists.

SEARCH AND FIND

★Trenton	E3	Newark	D5
Atlantic City	H4	Paterson	C5
Camden	F2	Vineland	G2
Jersey City	D5		

NEW JERSEY FACTS

Statehood Date (Order)	Area sq mi (sq km)	Population	Flower • Tree • Bird
December 18, 1787 (3rd)	7,787 (20,169)	8,717,925	Purple violet • Red oak • Eastern goldfinch

48

49

Fact boxes

You can use these statistics to discover the date that the state was admitted into the union as well as its area, population, flower, tree, and bird. On the region spreads, you will find the states in that region listed alphabetically, along with information on their highest and lowest elevations, state nicknames, and major rivers.

Physical maps

On these maps, you can find the towns where most people live as well as some areas that are important for other reasons, such as trade and tourism. The longest rivers, the highest mountains, and the most notable physical features are also shown.

Scale and compass

The scale allows you to find out how large an area is on a map. The compass shows you the direction of north.

Making Maps

About 4,500 years ago, a skilled worker in Babylon was making detailed markings on a clay tablet. The markings he made probably showed some buildings in a nearby river valley. The worker was making one of the very first maps. Today, most of our maps are produced by computers. Material is collected from surveys of Earth, aerial photos, and satellite images. Computers arrange this material to draw the highly accurate maps you use today.

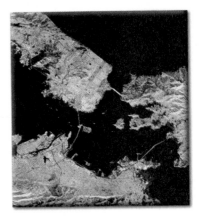

▲ *This is what San Francisco looks like when it is photographed from space.*

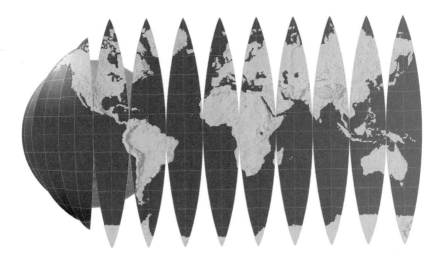

Peeling the orange

If you could peel off Earth's surface just like the skin of an orange, you would be left with segments similar to those shown here. Mapmakers who use this process fill the gaps in between the segments by digitally stretching them so that they form a flat surface.

What is a projection?

The fact that Earth is round means that mapmakers have a very difficult job representing it on a flat map. They have to stretch and distort Earth to make it appear flat on a page. The way in which Earth is stretched so it can appear on one page is called a *map projection*, and each map projection stretches the image of Earth in a different way. There are many different types of map projections, and the ones shown below are those most commonly used. Some map projections show the shape of the land accurately but distort the size. With others, the opposite is true. However, no map projection is completely accurate, and all of them distort to some extent.

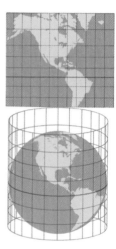 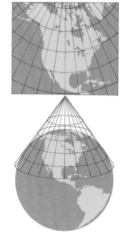 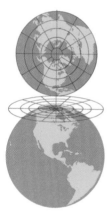

Cylinder shaped

Imagine wrapping a sheet of paper around a lit-up globe of the world and projecting the lines of latitude and longitude (see page 13) onto the paper. Unwrap the paper and spread it out flat to produce the kind of flat map often used by sailors.

Cone shaped

Imagine placing a paper cone over a lit-up globe and projecting the lines of latitude and longitude onto the cone. Unwrap and flatten it to produce the kind of map that shows wide areas of land, such as the United States or Russia.

Plane shaped

Imagine holding a sheet of paper so it touches one place on a lit-up globe. Project the lines of latitude and longitude onto the paper and then lay it on a flat surface. This kind of map is often used to show the world's polar regions.

Using Maps

A map is a picture of an area on Earth's surface. It uses lines, colors, and symbols to give you information about that area. It may be a picture of the whole world or of a small area in a city or town. Maps can tell you many different things, such as the location of countries, cities, and towns; the features of the landscape; the distribution of the population; or the climate of a particular region.

All about scale

The area shown on a map is, of course, much bigger than it appears on the printed page. This is because the map is drawn to scale. A map of the world shows us only a small amount of detail—we call it a *small-scale map*. A street map may show details of every building—it is called a *large-scale map*.

How to use a map scale

1 To measure the distance between two cities, first mark the positions of the city dots on the edge of a small piece of paper.

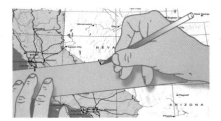

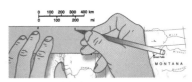

2 Place the paper along the map's scale, with the left-hand mark against the 0. If the scale is shorter than the distance you want to measure, mark where the scale ends, say 200 mi (320 km). Take a note of the distance you have already measured. Place this new mark against the 0.

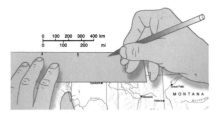

3 Repeat this last step until you have reached the mark for the second city. Then add up each of the distances. This will give you the correct total distance between the two cities.

Finding the location of a place

Maps are marked with a system of lines to help you describe and find the location of a certain place. The horizontal lines are called lines of latitude, and the vertical ones are lines of longitude. Latitude and longitude are measured in degrees (°).

Lines of latitude

These are imaginary lines that circle the world in an east–west direction. They tell you how far north or south a place is from the equator (a line drawn at 0° latitude.) They are drawn parallel to the equator. Two special lines of latitude are named the Tropic of Cancer and the Tropic of Capricorn. The Tropic of Cancer marks the northern boundary of the tropics, and the Tropic of Capricorn marks the southern boundary. Because these regions lie close to the equator, it is very hot, as the Sun shines directly overhead.

line of latitude

Tropic of Cancer
equator
Tropic of Capricorn

Lines of longitude

These are imaginary lines that run across Earth's surface in a north–south direction, from the North Pole to the South Pole. We start counting lines of longitude to the east and the west of the Greenwich Meridian, the 0° line of longitude that passes through the borough of Greenwich in London, England.

line of longitude

Hemispheres

The Greenwich Meridian and the 180° Meridian divide the world into two halves—the Eastern Hemisphere and the Western Hemisphere. Each hemisphere has 180 degrees of longitude.

Western Hemisphere

180° Meridian

Eastern Hemisphere

The equator divides the world into two halves, called the Northern Hemisphere and the Southern Hemisphere. Each hemisphere has 90 degrees of latitude.

Northern Hemisphere

equator

Southern Hemisphere

You can find any place on the surface of Earth on a map if you know its latitude and longitude. For example, the exact location of the city of Philadelphia, Pennsylvania, U.S.A., is as follows: 40°N, 75°W. In other words, Philadelphia lies on the line of latitude that is 40 degrees north of the equator, and on the line of longitude 75 degrees west of the Greenwich Meridian.

Weather and Climate

In the United States you may see lush green fields, windswept beaches, dry deserts, or humid swamps. Hawaii is warm and tropical, while Alaska is part of the frozen Arctic. Conditions are very different from one region to the next. Many things affect climate, such as how far north or south you are, how high above sea level, or how far from the ocean. The map here shows the main climate regions of the U.S.A. The east is generally mild or temperate; it is cooler in the north and warmer in the south. At the heart of the continent, there is less rainfall, with dry canyon lands and deserts lying between the Rocky Mountains and the coastal ranges of the west, which catch rainfall brought by ocean winds.

Alaska

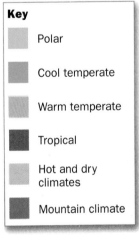

Key

Polar

Cool temperate

Warm temperate

Tropical

Hot and dry climates

Mountain climate

Hawaii

②

① Southeastern states have a warm climate, with heavy rainfall in the late summer and early fall. This feeds swamps and wetlands, such as Florida's Everglades.

② During the summer months, California's Death Valley is bone-dry and extremely hot, with an average temperature of 112°F (44°C).

③ Northern winters can be very cold with heavy snowfall. Blizzards can bring cities, such as Chicago, to a halt.

U.S.A. in a Day

Planet Earth actually spins around once every 23 hours 56 minutes and 4 seconds. The period from one dawn to the next is 24 hours, and we call that a day. Maine is the first state to receive the sun's rays each morning. The light spreads gradually across the nation's 6 time zones, brightens, and fades. Night falls and darkness once again covers the land. Just what happens to the United States and the 299 million people who live there in the course of a single day?

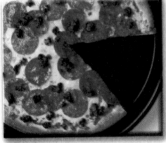

▲ Each day, Americans eat their way through 100 acres (41 ha) of pizza, enough to cover 77 football fields.

▲ In one day, about 6,480,008,358 gallons of water might flow over the various cascades that make up the spectacular Niagara Falls on the New York–Canadian border.

▼ In a typical day, about 11,600 cars are made in American factories.

▲ Each day, some 3,906,850 people travel on the New York City subway system, one of the world's busiest.

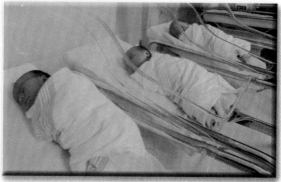

▶ Each day brings new life. More than 11,200 babies may be born in one average day in the U.S.A. Over the same period, about 6,700 Americans may be expected to die. Americans can expect to live to the age of 77.

◀ On average, about 275 thunderstorms take place in the U.S.A. every day. Daily weather conditions can vary greatly from one part of the country to another, and according to the season. Mount Waialeale in the state of Hawaii has more rainy days than anywhere else in the world—generally more than 350 in any year!

17

Time Zones

The United States covers 6 different time zones—Eastern, Central, Mountain, Pacific, Alaskan, and Hawaiian—each of which has a different time at any given moment. Time zones across the world are measured from a point that runs through the borough of Greenwich in London, England. The time at this point is known as Greenwich Mean Time (GMT). When it is 12 noon GMT, it is 7 a.m. U.S. Eastern Time, 6 a.m. U.S. Central Time, and so on.

Daylight Saving Time

In the spring, most of the country switches its clocks forward by one hour in order to save energy and make the most of daylight hours. This is called Daylight Saving Time (DST). DST starts at 2 a.m. on the second Sunday in March, and ends at 2 a.m. on the first Sunday in November. Hawaii and Arizona are the only places in the United States that do not observe DST.

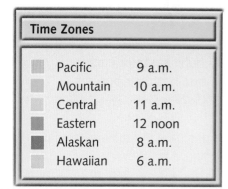

Time Zones

	Pacific	9 a.m.
	Mountain	10 a.m.
	Central	11 a.m.
	Eastern	12 noon
	Alaskan	8 a.m.
	Hawaiian	6 a.m.

① VERMONT
② NEW HAMPSHIRE
③ MASSACHUSETTS
④ CONNECTICUT
⑤ RHODE ISLAND
⑥ NEW JERSEY
⑦ DELAWARE
⑧ MARYLAND
★ WASHINGTON DC

States of the U.S.A.

This is a political map of the U.S.A., which names each
of the 50 states in the country and outlines their borders.

ALASKA

WASHINGTON

MONTANA

NORTH
DAKOTA

OREGON

IDAHO

SOUTH
DAKOTA

WYOMING

NEBRASKA

NEVADA

UTAH

COLORADO

KANSAS

OKLAHOM

CALIFORNIA

ARIZONA

NEW
MEXICO

HAWAII

TEXAS

U.S.A. FACTS

Number of states	50
Largest state by area	Alaska 591,004 sq mi (1,530,700 sq km)
Smallest state by area	Rhode Island 1,212 sq mi (3,140 sq km)
Total population	298,444,215
Largest state by population	California 36,132,147
Smallest state by population	Wyoming 509,294

① VERMONT
② NEW HAMPSHIRE
③ MASSACHUSETTS
④ CONNECTICUT
⑤ RHODE ISLAND
⑥ NEW JERSEY
⑦ DELAWARE
⑧ MARYLAND
★ WASHINGTON DC

The Physical U.S.A.

This map of the U.S.A. shows the main physical features of the country, including mountain ranges, plains, and major rivers.

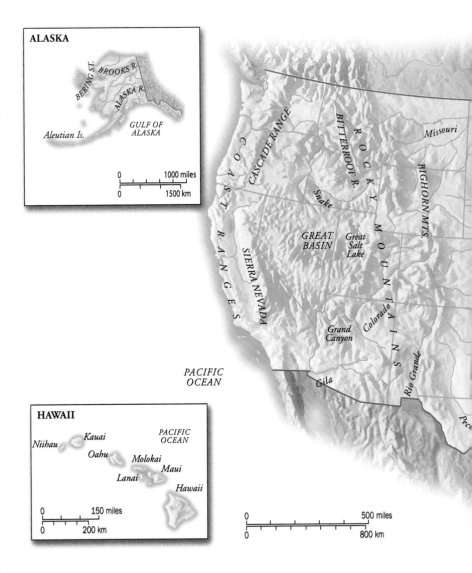

ALASKA

BERING ST.
BROOKS R.
ALASKA R.
Aleutian Is.
GULF OF ALASKA

0   1000 miles
0   1500 km

CASCADE RANGE
BITTERROOT R.
ROCKY
Missouri
COAST
Snake
BIGHORN MTS.
GREAT BASIN
Great Salt Lake
MOUNTAINS
RANGES
SIERRA NEVADA
Grand Canyon
Colorado
Rio Grande
PACIFIC OCEAN
Gila
Pec

HAWAII

Niihau
Kauai
Oahu
Molokai
Lanai
Maui
Hawaii
PACIFIC OCEAN

0   150 miles
0   200 km

0   500 miles
0   800 km

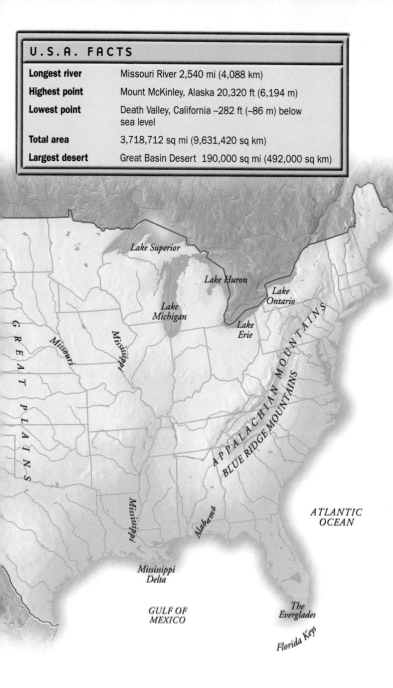

U.S.A. FACTS

Longest river	Missouri River 2,540 mi (4,088 km)
Highest point	Mount McKinley, Alaska 20,320 ft (6,194 m)
Lowest point	Death Valley, California –282 ft (–86 m) below sea level
Total area	3,718,712 sq mi (9,631,420 sq km)
Largest desert	Great Basin Desert 190,000 sq mi (492,000 sq km)

Lake Superior

Lake Huron

Lake Ontario

Lake Michigan

Lake Erie

G R E A T

Missouri

Mississippi

P L A I N S

A P P A L A C H I A N   M O U N T A I N S

BLUE RIDGE MOUNTAINS

Mississippi

Alabama

ATLANTIC OCEAN

Mississippi Delta

GULF OF MEXICO

The Everglades

Florida Keys

Alaska

United States

Hawaii

Northeast

The northeastern states stretch from the Great Lakes to the Atlantic Ocean and are crossed by hills, mountains, and farmland. This is a region of scenic old towns and villages, beautiful woodland, and mountains. The rocky North Atlantic coast runs southward to Long Island. New York State's green farmland, crossed by the Adirondack Mountains, stretches westward to the awesome Niagara Falls. Major cities include exciting, high-rise New York City and the historical seaport of Boston, Massachusetts.

SEARCH AND FIND

Connecticut	**New York**
Hartford F4	Albany E3
Maine	**Rhode Island**
Augusta D5	Providence F4
Massachusetts	**Vermont**
Boston E5	Montpelier D3
New Hampshire	
Concord E4	

REGION FACTS

	Highest elevation	Lowest elevation	State nickname	Major river(s)
Connecticut	Mount Frissell* 2,380 ft (725 m)	Sea level	Constitution State or Nutmeg State	Connecticut, Housatonic
Maine	Mount Katahdin 5,276 ft (1,608 m)	Sea level	Pine Tree State	Penobscot, St. John, Kennebec
Massachusetts	Mount Greylock 3,487 ft (1,062 m)	Sea level	Bay State or Old Colony State	Connecticut, Charles
New Hampshire	Mount Washington 6,288 ft (1,917 m)	Sea level	Granite State	Connecticut, Merrimack
New York	Mount Marcy 5,344 ft (1,629 m)	Sea level	Empire State	Hudson, Mohawk, Saint Lawrence
Rhode Island	Jenmoth Hill 812 ft (247 m)	Sea level	The Ocean State or Plantation State	Sakonnet
Vermont	Mount Mansfield 4,393 ft (1,339 m)	Lake Champlain 95 ft (29 m)	Green Mountain State	Connecticut, West, Otter

*Connecticut's highest elevation is actually an unnamed point at 2,380 ft (725 m) on the southern slopes of Mount Frissell. The summit of Mount Frissell is located in Massachusetts.

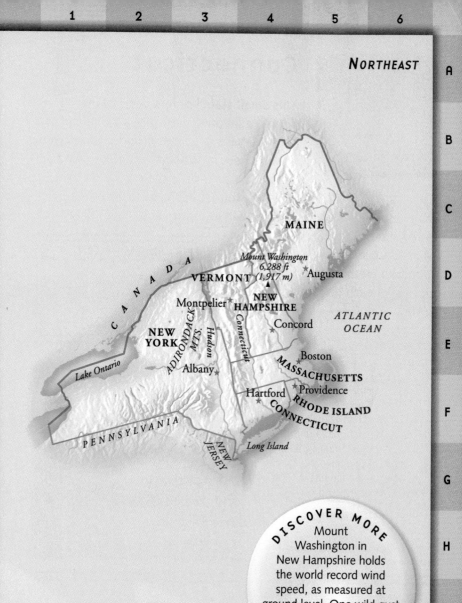

MAINE

Mount Washington
6,288 ft
(1,917 m)
▲

VERMONT

★ Augusta

NEW
HAMPSHIRE

Montpelier ★

ATLANTIC
OCEAN

★ Concord

NEW
YORK

ADIRONDACK MTS.

Hudson

Connecticut

Boston ★

MASSACHUSETTS

Lake Ontario

Albany ★

Hartford ★

★ Providence

RHODE ISLAND

CONNECTICUT

P E N N S Y L V A N I A

NEW
JERSEY

Long Island

C A N A D A

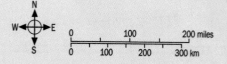

N
W ◆ E
S

0   100   200 miles
0   100   200   300 km

DISCOVER MORE
Mount
Washington in
New Hampshire holds
the world record wind
speed, as measured at
ground level. One wild gust
in 1934 measured an
incredible 231 mph
(372 kph).

25

Connecticut

This small state borders Long Island Sound, a favorite coast for yachting and fishing. Waterside cities include New Haven and Bridgeport. Woodland and farmland stretch toward hills in the northwest, which rise to 2,316 ft (706 m) at Bear Mountain. The state is home to many businesses and factories, with insurance companies based in the state capital, Hartford. Many people live in suburban areas of the state and travel each day to work in New York City.

SEARCH AND FIND

★Hartford	E3	New London	D4
Bridgeport	G4	Stamford	H5
Danbury	H4	Waterbury	G3
New Haven	F4		

DISCOVER MORE
Quinnehtukqut was Connecticut's original name. In the Mohican language that meant "beside the long tidal river." The Connecticut River is the longest in New England.

▶ *The gold-domed state capitol in Hartford was built in 1879.*

CONNECTICUT FACTS

Statehood Date (Order)	Area sq mi (sq km)	Population	Flower • Tree • Bird
January 9, 1788 (5TH)	5,018 (12,997)	3,510,297	Mountain laurel • White oak • Robin

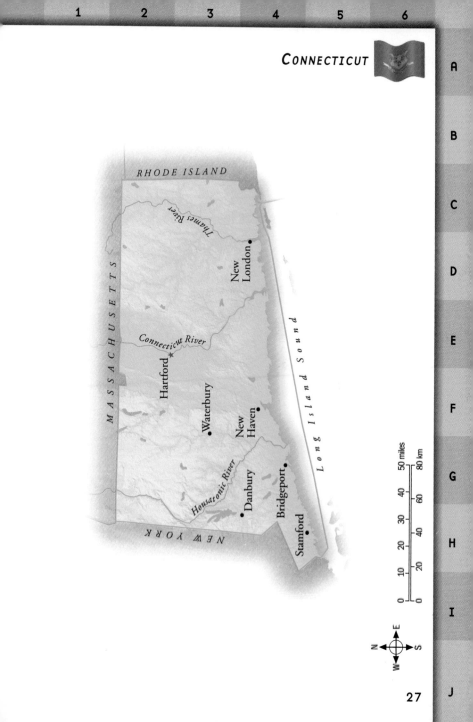

CONNECTICUT

Maine

Maine

South of the Canadian border lies Maine's rugged coastline, with its rocky inlets and tidal pools. Fishing and farming brought the first European settlers here, and the coast is still famous for its lobsters. Maine is thinly populated, even though it is the largest state in New England. It has many lakes, and forests whose leaves turn all shades of red and gold in the fall. Winters are icy. The largest city is Portland, a historic port on Casco Bay.

▶ *Lighthouses can be seen dotted along the coastline of Maine. They were built to guide ships such as whalers and clippers away from the treacherous rocky shores.*

DISCOVER MORE
Maine is the state for blueberries. It produces more of this sharp and juicy fruit than anywhere else in the United States. Small, wild varieties are a local speciality.

SEARCH AND FIND

★Augusta	.G2	Lewiston	.G2
Bangor	.F4	Portland	.H2
Biddeford	.H1	Waterville	.G3

MAINE FACTS

Statehood Date (Order)	Area sq mi (sq km)	Population	Flower • Tree • Bird
March 15, 1820 (23RD)	33,265 (86,156)	1,321,505	White pine cone and tassel • Eastern white pine • Chickadee

MAINE

CANADA

St. John River

CANADA

Mount Katahdin
5,267 ft (1,605 m)
▲

Moosehead
Lake

Penobscot River

Bangor ●

Waterville ●

NEW HAMPSHIRE

★ Augusta

Lewiston ●

Portland ●

Biddeford ●

*GULF OF
MAINE*

| 0 | 20 | 40 | 60 | 80 | 100 miles |
| 0 | 50 | 100 | | 150 km | |

N
W ◄◆► E
S

Massachusetts

Massachusetts

Boston is built around the shores of Massachusetts Bay. It is a historic city, set around a green area known as the Common. It is flanked by modern districts, roads, and tunnels. At Cape Cod, the coast curves out into the foggy Atlantic Ocean, like a big crab's claw. Woods and green fields lie inland. Farms produce apples, potatoes, and cranberries. Many of Massachusetts' towns and villages have a fascinating past, and students flock to the state's famous colleges.

DISCOVER MORE
Springfield, Massachusetts, has cold winters, so here, in 1898, Canadian-born James Naismith invented the world's first game of indoor basketball for his students.

◄ *Sailing is a popular pastime on the Charles River, which runs through the heart of Boston.*

SEARCH AND FIND

★Boston	D3	New Bedford	D4
Cambridge	E3	Pittsfield	I3
Fall River	E4	Springfield	G3
Lowell	E2	Worcester	F3

MASSACHUSETTS FACTS

Statehood Date (Order)	Area sq mi (sq km)	Population	Flower • Tree • Bird
February 6, 1788 (6TH)	8,284 (21,456)	6,398,743	Mayflower • American elm • Chickadee

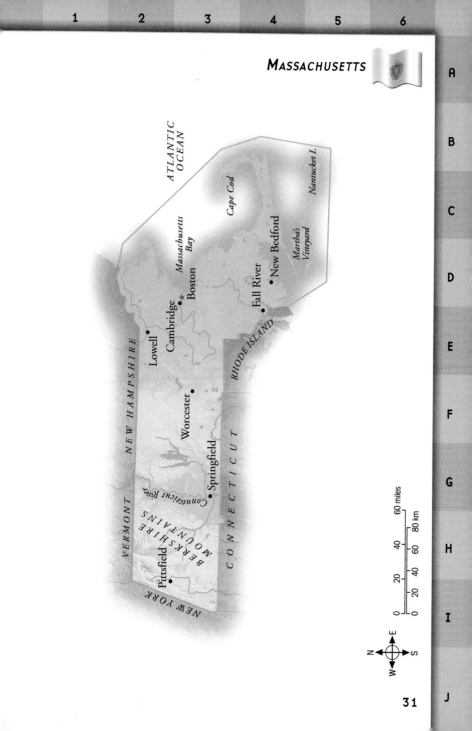

New Hampshire

New Hampshire

The state of New Hampshire lies between the Connecticut River and the Atlantic Ocean. The White Mountains rise to 6,288 ft (1,917 m) at Mount Washington, the highest point in the region. The mountains are flanked by beautiful woodland, lakes, and streams. Here, there was never any shortage of timber or stone for building, or water for powering mills, so the region attracted industry in the early days of American history. Today's factories make machinery, textiles, and leather goods. Farm produce includes apples, hay, and vegetables.

SEARCH AND FIND

★Concord	.....H3	Manchester	....H4
Conway	.......F5	Nashua	.......I4
Dover	........H5	Portsmouth	....H6
Keene	........H1	Rochester	.....G5

▼ New Hampshire is known for its covered bridges. Swift River Bridge in Conway was constructed in 1870.

DISCOVER MORE
Europeans first settled in New Hampshire in 1623. New Hampshire was first to claim its freedom from the British. It declared independence before the other original 13 colonies.

NEW HAMPSHIRE FACTS

Statehood Date (Order)	Area sq mi (sq km)	Population	Flower • Tree • Bird
June 21, 1788 (9TH)	9,279 (24,032)	1,309,940	Purple lilac • White birch • Purple finch

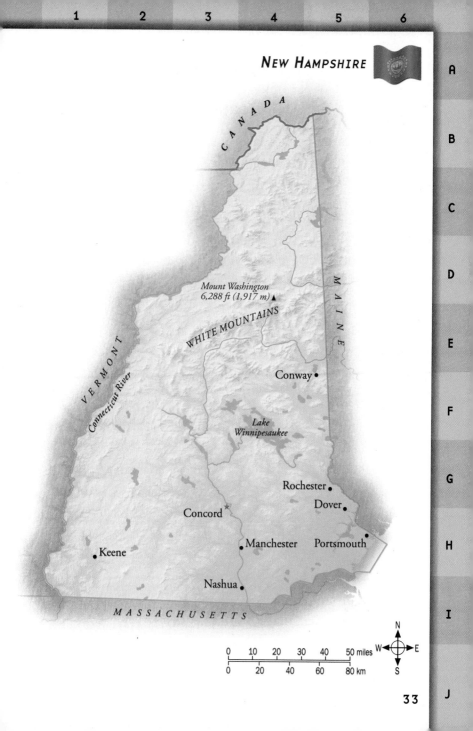

| | 1 | 2 | 3 | 4 | 5 | 6 |

A

B

CANADA

C

D

MAINE

Mount Washington
6,288 ft (1,917 m) ▲

WHITE MOUNTAINS

E

VERMONT

Conway •

Connecticut River

F

Lake
Winnipesaukee

G

Rochester •

Concord ☆

Dover •

H

Manchester •

Portsmouth •

Keene •

Nashua •

I

MASSACHUSETTS

0 10 20 30 40 50 miles

0   20   40   60   80 km

N
W ◆ E
S

J

New York

New York City's towers of glass and concrete soar skyward from the island of Manhattan, between the Hudson and East rivers. The city is home to the theater district of Broadway, the financial center of Wall Street, and the long, green strip of Central Park. The rest of New York State stretches westward to the Adirondack and Catskill mountains. This is a different world, with peaceful green fields grazed by dairy cattle. Lakeside cities include Rochester, famous for its imaging and copying industries, and Buffalo, a center of biological and genetic research.

▶ *Niagara Falls sits on the border between New York State and Ontario, Canada. There are two falls—the American Falls (shown here in the foreground) and the Horseshoe Falls, which lie in Canada.*

DISCOVER MORE

New York City is the most crowded spot in North America. Some 18.6 million people live in the city and its surrounding areas, with more than 8 million living in the city itself.

SEARCH AND FIND

★Albany	D3	Poughkeepsie	D4
Binghampton	F4	Rochester	G3
Buffalo	H3	Schenectady	D3
New York City	D5	Syracuse	F3
Niagara Falls	I3	Utica	E3

NEW YORK FACTS

Statehood Date (Order)	Area sq mi (sq km)	Population	Flower • Tree • Bird
July 26, 1788 (11TH)	49,108 (127,190)	19,254,630	Rose • Sugar maple • Bluebird

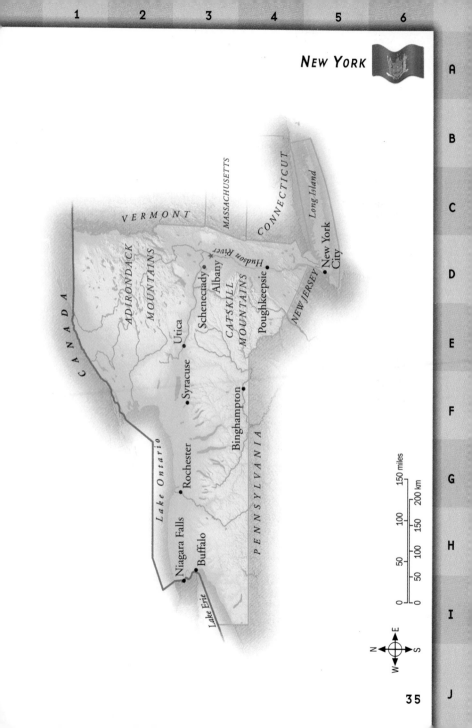

NEW YORK

CANADA

VERMONT

MASSACHUSETTS

CONNECTICUT

Long Island

ADIRONDACK
MOUNTAINS

Hudson River

New York
City

Schenectady
Albany

Utica

CATSKILL
MOUNTAINS

Poughkeepsie

NEW JERSEY

Syracuse

Binghampton

Lake Ontario

Rochester

PENNSYLVANIA

Niagara Falls
Buffalo

Lake Erie

150 miles
200 km

100
150

50
100

0   50

0   0

N
W — E
S

Rhode Island

Rhode Island

Rhode Island is the smallest state in the nation. Its low-lying mainland drains into the Blackstone River. This flows, in turn, into Narrangansett Bay, amid a maze of small islands. The state's wealth comes from textiles, boatbuilding, metalworking, electrical engineering, and machinery. The biggest center of population is the city of Providence. Rhode Island also includes attractive countryside and coastal areas. Sailing is a popular pastime for the wealthy in Newport. Tourists come to Newport to see the big mansions, walk along the cliffs and beaches, taste the clam chowder, or visit the popular jazz festivals.

◀ This 70-room palatial home is one of the many mansions in Newport that are open to the public. It was built for the wealthy Vanderbilt family in 1895.

SEARCH AND FIND

★Providence	C4	Pawtucket	C4
Cranston	D4	Warwick	E4
Newport	F5	Westerly	G1

DISCOVER MORE

You are never more than 30 mi (48 km) from the salty ocean when you are in Rhode Island. That is why it has been given its nickname, the Ocean State.

RHODE ISLAND FACTS

Statehood Date (Order)	Area sq mi (sq km)	Population	Flower • Tree • Bird
May 29, 1790 (13TH)	1,212 (3,140)	1,076,189	Violet • Red maple • Rhode Island red

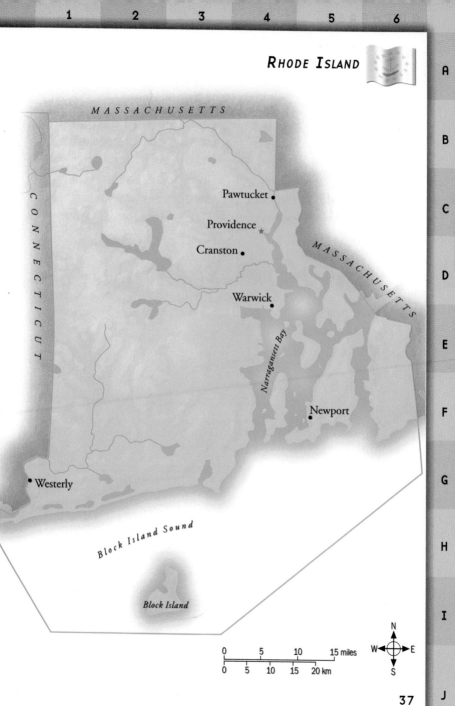

RHODE ISLAND

MASSACHUSETTS

Pawtucket

Providence

Cranston

MASSACHUSETTS

CONNECTICUT

Warwick

Narragansett Bay

Newport

Westerly

Block Island Sound

Block Island

| 0 | 5 | 10 | 15 miles |

| 0 | 5 | 10 | 15 | 20 km |

N
W ← → E
S

Vermont

Vermont

Vermont borders the Canadian province of Quebec. The Green Mountains, a northern range of the Appalachians, are popular with visitors. Tourists take advantage of the heavy winter snowfall for skiing, and they view trees changing color in the fall. Sugar maple trees provide a sweet, sticky sap, used to make maple syrup. The peaceful rural state of Vermont has villages with white churches, wooden houses, and cattle farms. Montpelier is the smallest state capital in the nation, with a population of less than 10,000.

▲ Trees covered in orange and red leaves, a typical sight in Vermont in the fall, form a backdrop to this picturesque rural village in the state.

DISCOVER MORE

The name *Vermont* comes from the French *vert*, meaning "green" and *mont*, meaning "mount." It was made up by French Canadian pioneers.

SEARCH AND FIND

★Montpelier . . .D3	Burlington D1
Barre E3	Rutland F2
Bennington I1	Springfield G3

VERMONT FACTS

Statehood Date (Order)	Area sq mi (sq km)	Population	Flower • Tree • Bird
March 4, 1791 (14TH)	9,614 (24,900)	623,050	Red clover • Sugar maple • Hermit thrush

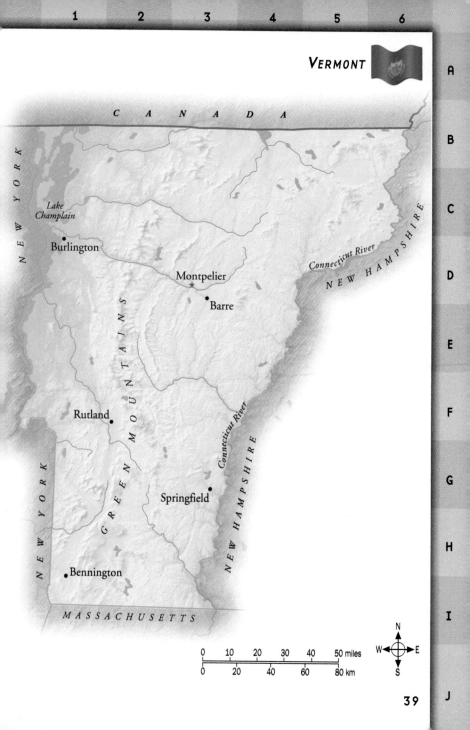

Alaska

United States

Hawaii

Mid-Atlantic

The Mid-Atlantic, or central eastern states, lie between Lake Erie and the Atlantic Ocean. Lots of people live in the towns and suburbs of New Jersey, working in factories, offices, and seaside resorts. Pennsylvania stretches west from the Delaware River all the way to Lake Erie. The Atlantic coast has two long inlets, one at Delaware Bay and one at Chesapeake Bay, with its port of Baltimore, Maryland. Foothills rise to the Appalachian Mountains. Beside the Potomac River is the national capital, Washington DC, which is home to over 5 million people.

DISCOVER MORE

Pennsylvania's Punxsutawney Phil is a famous groundhog. Tradition says that if he sees his own shadow on February 2, Groundhog Day, six more weeks of winter follow.

SEARCH AND FIND

Delaware
Dover F5

District of Columbia
Washington. F4

Maryland
Annapolis F4

New Jersey
Trenton E5

Pennysylvania
Harrisburg. E3

REGION FACTS

	Highest elevation	Lowest elevation	State nickname	Major river(s)
Delaware	Ebright Road 450 ft (137 m)	Sea level	First State or Diamond State	Delaware, Mispillion, Nanticoke
District of Columbia	Tenleytown 410 ft (125 m)	Sea level	none	Potomac
Maryland	Backbone Mountain 3,360 ft (1,024 m)	Sea level	Free State or Old Line State	Potomac, Patapsco, Susquehanna
New Jersey	High Point 1,803 ft (550 m)	Sea level	Garden State	Delaware, Hudson
Pennsylvania	Mount Davis 3,213 ft (979 m)	Sea level along Delaware River	Keystone State	Delaware, Allegheny, Susquehanna

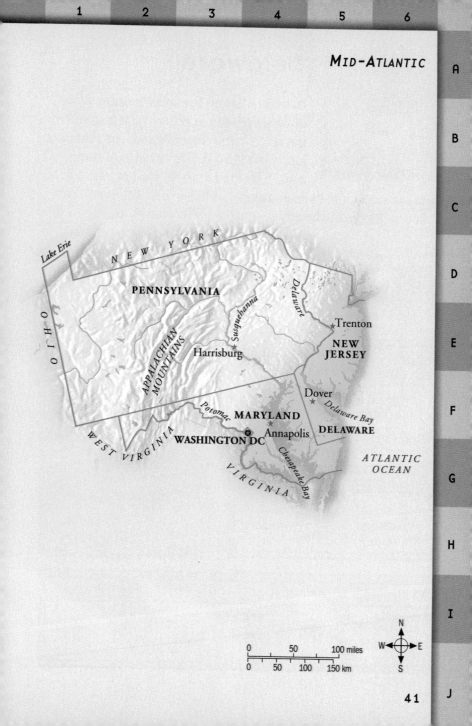

1 2 3 4 5 6

A

B

C

D

E

F

G

H

I

J

Lake Erie

NEW YORK

PENNSYLVANIA

OHIO

APPALACHIAN MOUNTAINS

Susquehanna

Delaware

Trenton

NEW JERSEY

Harrisburg

Dover

Delaware Bay

WEST VIRGINIA

Potomac

MARYLAND

Annapolis

DELAWARE

WASHINGTON DC

VIRGINIA

Chesapeake Bay

ATLANTIC OCEAN

0   50   100 miles
0   50   100   150 km

N
W ✦ E
S

Delaware

Delaware lies on the southwestern shore of Delaware Bay. It is the smallest state in the U.S.A. after Rhode Island, and measures just 96 mi (154 km) from north to south, and 35 mi (56 km) from west to east. Its state capital, Dover, is the location of a major U.S. Air Force base. Delaware produces chemicals, construction materials, plastics, and electronics. The ocean coast has sandy beaches and tourist resorts, such as Bethany Beach, Rehoboth Beach, and Lewes.

DISCOVER MORE

Delaware is known as the "First State" because it was the first to ratify, or confirm, the U.S. Constitution, on December 7, 1787. This date is featured on the state flag.

▶ *Delaware Memorial Bridge, linking Delaware to New Jersey, is the world's longest twin-span bridge.*

SEARCH AND FIND

★Dover	.E2	Rehoboth Beach	G5
Milford City.	.F3	Seaford.	.H2
Newark	.B1	Wilmington.	.B2

DELAWARE FACTS

Statehood Date (Order)	Area sq mi (sq km)	Population	Flower • Tree • Bird
December 7, 1787 (1ST)	2,045 (5,295)	843,524	Peach blossom • American holly • Blue hen chicken

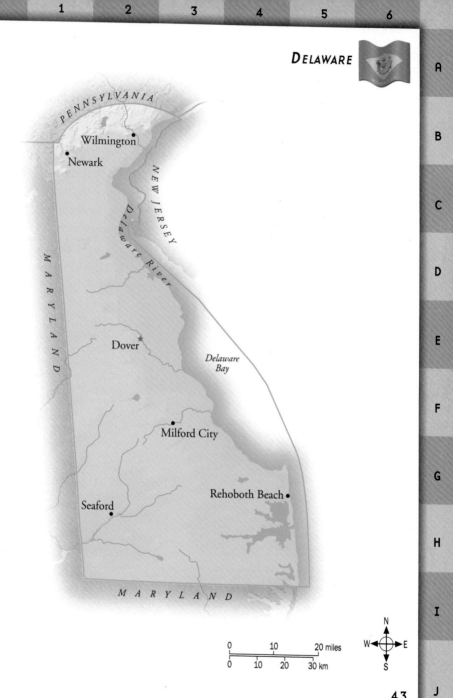

DELAWARE

PENNSYLVANIA

Wilmington

Newark

NEW JERSEY

Delaware River

MARYLAND

Dover

Delaware Bay

Milford City

Rehoboth Beach

Seaford

MARYLAND

0   10   20 miles
0   10   20   30 km

N
W ← ⊕ → E
S

District of
Columbia

District of Columbia

The District of Columbia (DC) is not in any state. It is territory set aside for the federal capital. It occupies 68 sq mi (177 sq km) on the banks of the Potomac River. Most of DC is taken up by the city of Washington, whose leafy avenues and parks are visited by millions of tourists each year. Here is Capitol Hill, home of Congress and the Supreme Court, and the National Mall, which features many monuments.

Nearby, the White House is the impressive residence and office of the U.S. President.

◀ *The Congress of the United States meets in the Capitol building, which is situated on Capitol Hill in Washington.*

DISCOVER MORE
The Library of Congress is the world's largest library, containing 130 million items, including 29 million books. The total length of the shelves runs for about 530 mi (853 km).

SEARCH AND FIND

Capitol. E3	Supreme Court. .E4
National Mall . . .E3	White House. . . .E3

DISTRICT OF COLUMBIA FACTS

Statehood Date (Order)	Area sq mi (sq km)	Population	Flower • Tree • Bird
none	69 (178)	550,521	American Beauty rose • Scarlet oak • Woodthrush

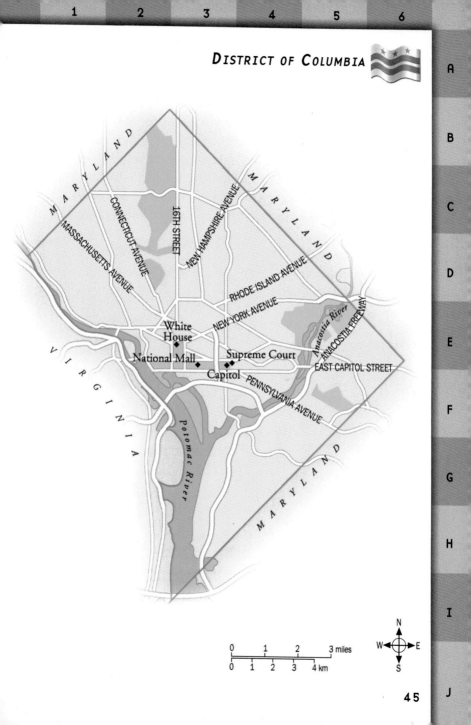

1 2 3 4 5 6

DISTRICT OF COLUMBIA

A

B

M A R Y L A N D

M A R Y L A N D

C

MASSACHUSETTS AVENUE

CONNECTICUT AVENUE

16TH STREET

NEW HAMPSHIRE AVENUE

D

RHODE ISLAND AVENUE

NEW YORK AVENUE

White House

V I R G I N I A

National Mall

Supreme Court

E

Capitol

Anacostia River

ANACOSTIA FREEWAY

EAST CAPITOL STREET

PENNSYLVANIA AVENUE

F

P o t o m a c   R i v e r

M A R Y L A N D

G

H

I

0   1   2   3 miles

0   1   2   3   4 km

N
W ⊕ E
S

J

45

Maryland

Maryland

Long, sandy beaches border the Atlantic coast of Maryland. Most of the state is made up of the ragged coastline of Chesapeake Bay, famous for its soft-shell blue crabs, and surrounding farmland and fishing villages. A long, narrow strip of land reaches westward along the Potomac River toward the Appalachian Mountains.

Maryland's largest city is Baltimore, one of the most important seaports on the Atlantic coast and a center of the pharmaceutical industry.

▶ *Maryland's famous blue crabs have provided a valuable source of income in the state since the mid-1800s.*

DISCOVER MORE

Assateague Island is home to a famous breed of wild ponies. Some say that they are descendants of animals that swam ashore from a Spanish shipwreck in the 1500s.

SEARCH AND FIND

★Annapolis	D2	Cumberland	H1
Baltimore	D2	Frederick	F2
Chestertown	D2	Gaithersburg	E2
Columbia	E2	Hagerstown	F1

MARYLAND FACTS

Statehood Date (Order)	Area sq mi (sq km)	Population	Flower • Tree • Bird
April 28, 1788 (7TH)	10,460 (27,092)	5,600,388	Black-eyed Susan • White oak • Baltimore oriole

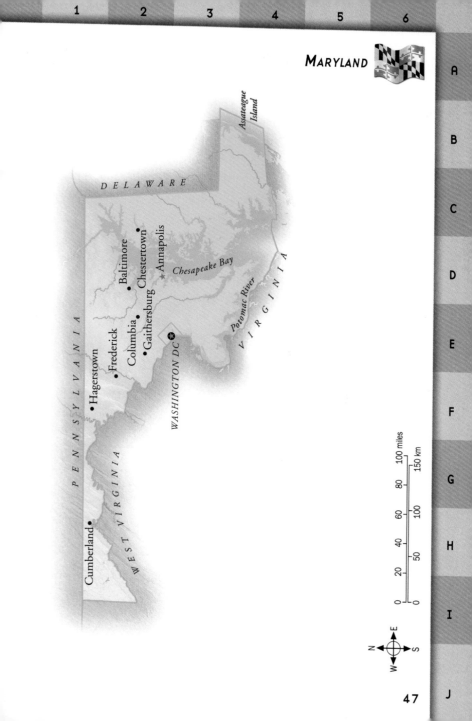

MARYLAND

1 2 3 4 5 6

A B C D E F G H I J

Assateague Island

DELAWARE

Baltimore
Chestertown
Annapolis
Chesapeake Bay

Frederick
Columbia
Gaithersburg

WASHINGTON DC

Hagerstown

PENNSYLVANIA

WEST VIRGINIA

Cumberland

Potomac River

VIRGINIA

0   20   40   60   80   100 miles
0   50   100 150 km

N E S W

New Jersey

New Jersey

The coastal state of New Jersey lies between the Delaware River in the west and Delaware Bay in the south. Its Atlantic shore is sandy, with areas of lagoons and marsh as well as seaside resorts such as Atlantic City. A central plateau rises to hills in the northwest. New Jersey's crops include tomatoes, peaches, and apples. The state has many cities, such as Newark and Trenton. Industries include oil refining, chemicals, and electrical engineering.

DISCOVER MORE

The state of New Jersey is the most densely populated in the whole of the United States. It is home to 1,134 people per sq mi (438 per sq km).

◀ Point Pleasant Beach is one of many resorts along the New Jersey Shore that are popular with tourists.

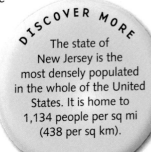

SEARCH AND FIND

★Trenton E3	Newark D5
Atlantic City H4	Paterson C5
Camden F2	Vineland G2
Jersey City D5	

NEW JERSEY FACTS

Statehood Date (Order)	Area sq mi (sq km)	Population	Flower • Tree • Bird
December 18, 1787 (3RD)	7,787 (20,169)	8,717,925	Purple violet • Red oak • Eastern goldfinch

NEW JERSEY

1 2 3 4 5 6

A B C D E F G H I J

PENNSYLVANIA

Delaware River

NEW YORK

Paterson

Jersey
City

NEW YORK

Newark

Delaware River

★ Trenton

PENNSYLVANIA

Camden

ATLANTIC
OCEAN

Delaware River

PINE
BARRENS

D E L A W A R E

Vineland

Atlantic
City

*Delaware
Bay*

N
W ← → E
S

0   10   20   30   40   50 miles

0   20   40   60   80 km

Pennsylvania

Pennsylvania

Pennsylvania lies between the Delaware River in the east and the shores of Lake Erie in the northwest. The state is crossed by the Appalachian and Allegheny mountains and the Allegheny Plateau. This is a landscape of forests and farms, with reserves of coal. Its two big cities are at opposite ends of the state. Pittsburgh in the west grew up as a steel-producing city, but now has turned to modern industries such as robotics. Historic Philadelphia in the east is a center of business, with its own stock exchange.

▶ Philadelphia's Liberty Bell most famously rang in July 1776, calling people to hear the first public reading of the U.S. Declaration of Independence.

DISCOVER MORE

Many of Pennsylvania's Amish religious community live in Lancaster County. They wear traditional clothes and aim to lead a plain and simple life.

SEARCH AND FIND

★Harrisburg	. . .E4	Lancaster	. . . . . .D4
Allentown	. . . . . .C3	Philadelphia	. . . .C4
Altoona	. . . . . . .G3	Pittsburgh	. . . . . .I3
Erie	. . . . .I1	Reading	. . . . . .D3
Gettysburg	. . . . .E4	Scranton	. . . . . .D2

PENNSYLVANIA FACTS

Statehood Date (Order)	Area sq mi (sq km)	Population	Flower • Tree • Bird
December 12, 1787 (2ND)	45,308 (117,348)	12,429,616	Mountain laurel • Hemlock • Ruffed grouse

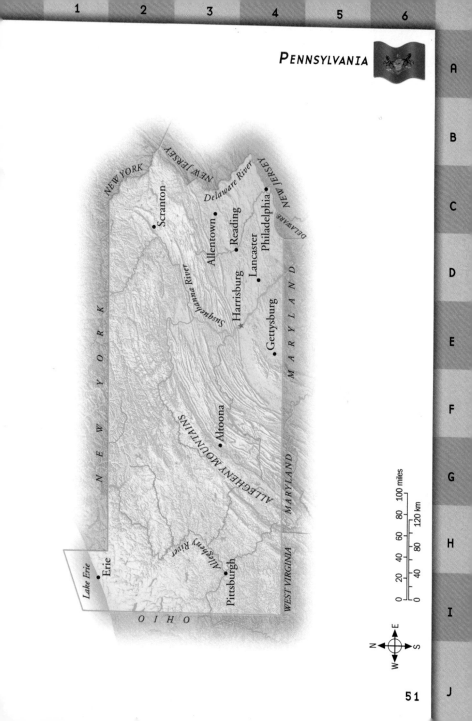

1 2 3 4 5 6

A B C D E F G H I J

NEW YORK

NEW JERSEY

Delaware River

Scranton

Allentown
Reading
Lancaster
Philadelphia

NEW JERSEY

DELAWARE

Susquehanna River

Harrisburg

Gettysburg

MARYLAND

MARYLAND

NEW YORK

ALLEGHENY MOUNTAINS

Altoona

Allegheny River

WEST VIRGINIA

Lake Erie

Erie

Pittsburgh

OHIO

0   20   40   60   80   100 miles
0   40   80   120 km

N E W S

Deep South

Alaska

United States

Hawaii

The states of the Deep South border the Gulf of Mexico and the Atlantic Ocean. Hurricane season occurs in late summer and fall and can sometimes cause floods and a lot of destruction. In the east are the states of Alabama and Georgia. Tourists and fishermen flock to the sunny peninsula of Florida, with its low-lying sandy islands, called "keys." The muddy waters of the Mississippi River cross the western part of the region, flowing through the city of New Orleans, Louisiana. The river's delta is a center of the oil industry, while southern farms across the region grow peanuts, rice, peaches, onions, and cotton. West of the Mississippi lies the scenic state of Arkansas.

SEARCH AND FIND

Alabama	**Georgia**
Montgomery . . .D3	Atlanta D4
Arkansas	**Louisiana**
Little Rock. D1	Baton Rouge . . .E2
Florida	**Mississippi**
Tallahassee E4	Jackson. D2

REGION FACTS

	Highest elevation	Lowest elevation	State nickname	Major river(s)
Alabama	Cheaha Mountain 2,407 ft (734 m)	Sea level	Cotton State or Heart of Dixie	Alabama, Tennessee, Chattahoochee
Arkansas	Magazine Mountain 2,753 ft (839 m)	Ouachita River 55 ft (17 m)	The Natural State or Wonder State	Mississippi, White, Arkansas
Florida	Britton Hill 345 ft (105 m)	Sea level	Sunshine State or Peninsula State	Apalachicola, Suwannee
Georgia	Brasstown Bald 4,784 ft (1,458 m)	Sea level	Peach State	Savannah, Ogeechee Chattahoochee
Louisiana	Driskill Mountain 535 ft (163 m)	New Orleans −8 ft (−2.4 m)	Pelican State or Creole State	Mississippi, Red, Ouachita
Mississippi	Woodall Mountain 806 ft (246 m)	Sea level	Magnolia State	Mississippi, Pearl, Yazoo

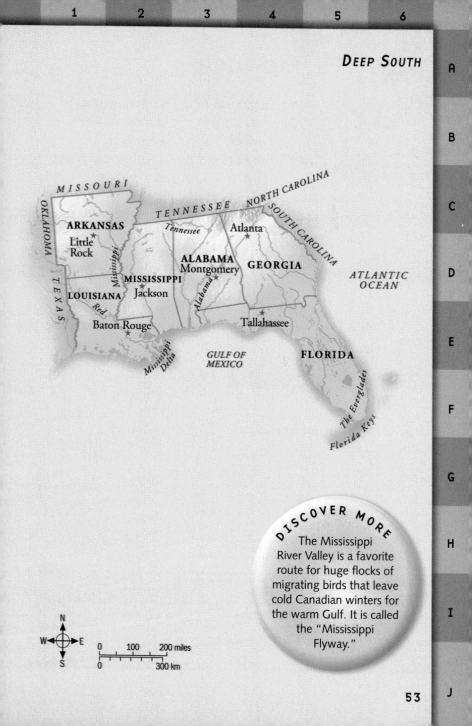

1 2 3 4 5 6

A

B

C

MISSOURI

OKLAHOMA

ARKANSAS
Little
Rock ★

TENNESSEE   *NORTH CAROLINA*

Tennessee

Atlanta ★

SOUTH CAROLINA

ALABAMA
Montgomery ★

GEORGIA

D

T E X A S

MISSISSIPPI
Jackson ★

LOUISIANA

Mississippi

Red

Alabama

ATLANTIC
OCEAN

Baton Rouge ★

Tallahassee ★

*Mississippi
Delta*

GULF OF
MEXICO

FLORIDA

E

F

The Everglades

Florida Keys

G

DISCOVER MORE
The Mississippi
River Valley is a favorite
route for huge flocks of
migrating birds that leave
cold Canadian winters for
the warm Gulf. It is called
the "Mississippi
Flyway."

H

I

N
W ◈ E
S

0   100   200 miles

0   300 km

J

Alabama

The Cumberland Plateau, in northern Alabama, is a region of lakes and white-water rapids. The Tennessee River crosses the state border. Central Alabama is made up of farmland producing corn, cotton, and peanuts. Birmingham was founded as a city for manufacturing iron and steel. It now relies more on service industries, such as medical research and publishing. The state capital is Montgomery, a city of more than 200,000 people. The Alabama River flows south toward Mobile Bay, on a narrow strip of the hot, humid Gulf coast.

▲ *The Battleship USS* Alabama *Memorial Park is in Mobile, on the Gulf of Mexico. Here, visitors can board the ship and a submarine named* Drum.

DISCOVER MORE
The city of Huntsville, in northern Alabama, is home to the U.S. Space Camp, which offers a variety of programs in which children can study space, aviation, and robotics.

SEARCH AND FIND

★Montgomery . .F4	Gadsden D4
Birmingham D3	Huntsville C3
Decatur C3	Mobile I1
Dothan H5	Tuscaloosa E2

ALABAMA FACTS

Statehood Date (Order)	Area sq mi (sq km)	Population	Flower • Tree • Bird
December 14, 1819 (22ND)	51,705 (133,915)	4,557,808	Camellia • Southern pine • Yellowhammer

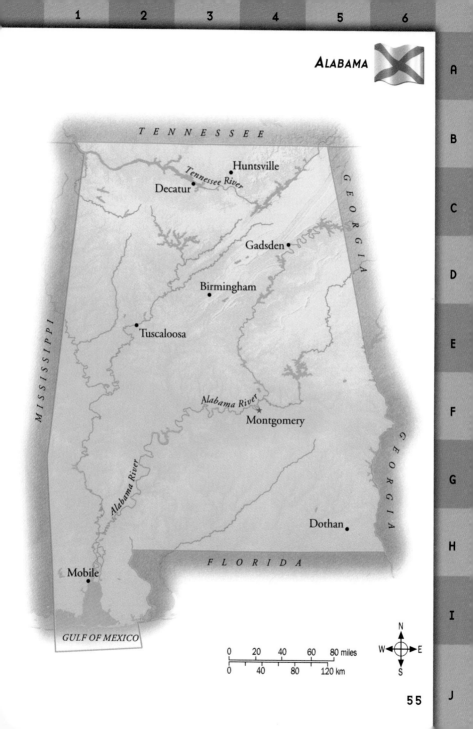

Arkansas

Arkansas lies to the west of the Mississippi River, on the edge of the Great Plains. The state is divided in two by the Arkansas River, which flows through the state capital, Little Rock. To the west of the river are the forests of the Ozark Plateau and the Boston and Ouachita mountain ranges. To the east of the river lies farmland, which produces cotton, soybeans, and poultry. The state is also one of the biggest rice producers in the U.S.A. Bauxite, a metal ore, is mined in Arkansas and is used for making chemicals and polishes.

SEARCH AND FIND

★Little Rock . . . .F3   Jonesboro D1
Fayetteville . . . . .H1   Pine Bluff E4
Fort Smith . . . . .H2   Texarkana H4
Hot Springs . . . .G3   West Memphis . .C2

▼ The State Capitol in Little Rock is based on the U.S. Capitol building in Washington DC.

DISCOVER MORE

Arkansas is named after one of the Native American nations. It is the only state with a law telling people how to pronounce its name (AR-kan-SAW)!

ARKANSAS FACTS

Statehood Date (Order)	Area sq mi (sq km)	Population	Flower • Tree • Bird
June 15, 1836 (25TH)	53,187 (137,754)	2,779,154	Apple blossom • Pine • Mockingbird

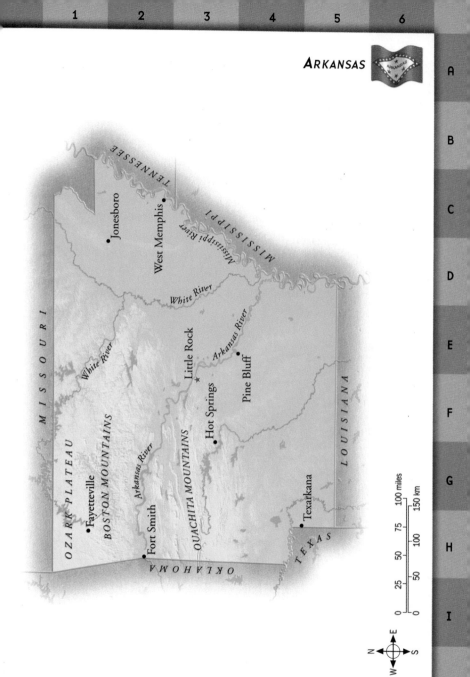

ARKANSAS

| 1 | 2 | 3 | 4 | 5 | 6 |

A
B
C
D
E
F
G
H
I
J

TENNESSEE

MISSISSIPPI

Jonesboro

West Memphis

Mississippi River

White River

MISSOURI

White River

Little Rock

Arkansas River

Pine Bluff

OZARK PLATEAU

BOSTON MOUNTAINS

Fayetteville

Arkansas River

OUACHITA MOUNTAINS

Hot Springs

LOUISIANA

Fort Smith

Texarkana

OKLAHOMA

TEXAS

100 miles
150 km
75
100
50
50
25
50
0
0

N E S W

57

Florida

Florida forms a long, narrow peninsula.
It separates the Gulf of Mexico from the Atlantic Ocean and ends in a chain of small islands, called the Florida Keys. A huge wetland area stretches south from Lake Okeechobee to the Everglades National Park. Florida's subtropical climate allows citrus fruits to be a major crop. The sunshine also attracts tourists, golfers, and retired people. Major centers of population include the sprawling city of Jacksonville and rapidly growing Miami, which many Latin American and Caribbean immigrants have made their home. On the east coast is the famous John F. Kennedy Space Center.

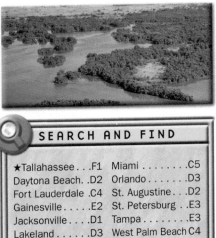

▶ The Everglades are made up of many small islands. The swamps are home to a large variety of animals and plant life.

DISCOVER MORE
St. Augustine was the first full-time European settlement in the U.S.A. It dates back to 1565 and was founded by a Spanish adventurer named Pedro Menéndez de Avilés.

SEARCH AND FIND

★Tallahassee	F1	Miami	C5
Daytona Beach	D2	Orlando	D3
Fort Lauderdale	C4	St. Augustine	D2
Gainesville	E2	St. Petersburg	E3
Jacksonville	D1	Tampa	E3
Lakeland	D3	West Palm Beach	C4

FLORIDA FACTS

Statehood Date (Order)	Area sq mi (sq km)	Population	Flower • Tree • Bird
March 3, 1845 (27TH)	58,664 (151,939)	17,789,864	Orange blossom • Sabal palm • Mockingbird

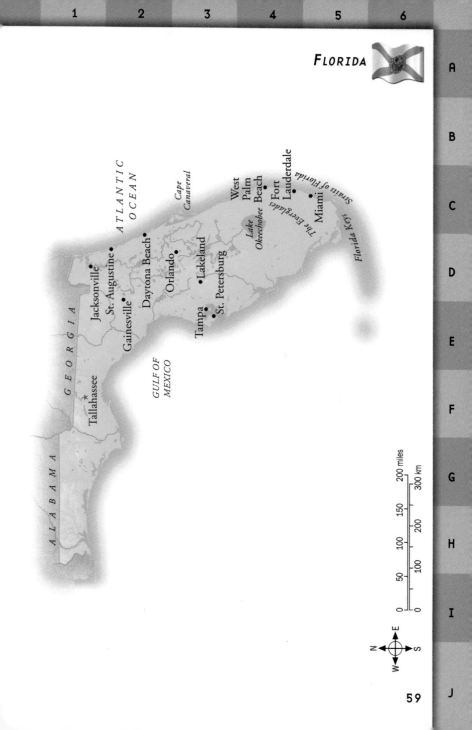

Georgia

Georgia's swampy, low-lying coast borders the Atlantic Ocean. The chief seaport is Savannah. Farther west, land rises to the Piedmont Plateau and the southern mountains of the Appalachian range.

Georgia's soil is a clay, colored red by iron. It is planted with cotton, onions, corn, peanuts, and pecans, and its orchards are famous for their peaches. The state capital is Atlanta, a city of 4.6 million people. Burned down during the Civil War, Atlanta was rebuilt and became an industrial giant. Atlanta is a center of business, especially in the areas of airlines, television, and soft drinks.

▲ Atlanta used to be called Terminus because it was at the end of a railroad. It became Atlanta in 1845.

DISCOVER MORE

Georgia's Blackbeard Island is named for the fearsome pirate Edward Teach, known as "Blackbeard." Legend says he buried his treasure on the island in the early 1700s.

SEARCH AND FIND

★Atlanta	E2	Columbus	F1
Albany	G2	Macon	F3
Athens	D3	Savannah	G6

GEORGIA FACTS

Statehood Date (Order)	Area sq mi (sq km)	Population	Flower • Tree • Bird
January 2, 1788 (4TH)	58,910 (152,576)	9,072,576	Cherokee rose • Live oak • Brown thrasher

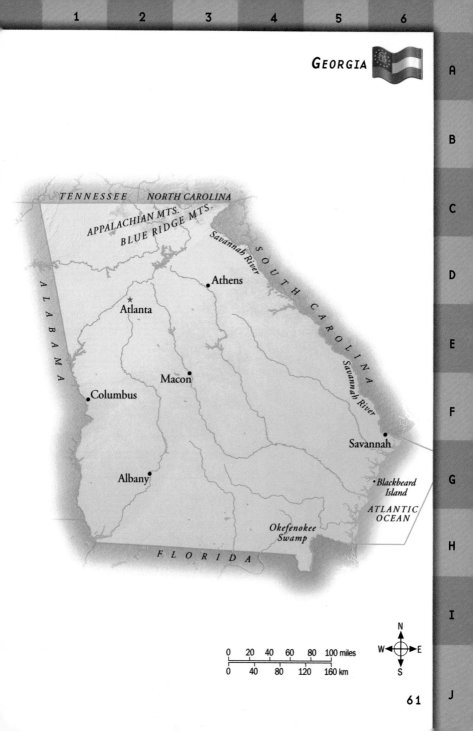

GEORGIA

TENNESSEE   NORTH CAROLINA

APPALACHIAN MTS.
BLUE RIDGE MTS.

Savannah River

SOUTH CAROLINA

Athens

★ Atlanta

ALABAMA

Macon

Columbus

Savannah River

Savannah

Albany

Blackbeard
Island

ATLANTIC
OCEAN

Okefenokee
Swamp

FLORIDA

0 20 40 60 80 100 miles

0   40   80   120   160 km

N
W ◆ E
S

Louisiana

Louisiana

Louisiana is a low-lying state. The climate is often hot and sticky, with thunder, rain, and hurricanes in late summer. The wide waters of the Mississippi River form the northeastern state border. Its course is lined with high embankments, called levees. The river rolls on to the coast through the city of New Orleans, which is the birthplace of jazz music. The city is also famous for gumbo, which is a spicy okra stew, often made with seafood. Louisiana grows soybeans, cotton, sugarcane, and rice. The state is also a center of the oil industry.

▶ *Every February or March, New Orleans hosts a Mardi Gras festival with colorful street parades.*

DISCOVER MORE
Louisiana has huge areas of marshes, swamps, ponds, and bayous (creeks). These make an ideal home for alligators. There are around 1 million of these giant reptiles in the state.

SEARCH AND FIND

★Baton Rouge . .E4	Monroe F1
Alexandria G3	New Orleans . . .D4
Lafayette F4	Shreveport H1
Lake Charles . . .G4	

LOUISIANA FACTS

Statehood Date (Order)	Area sq mi (sq km)	Population	Flower • Tree • Bird
April 30, 1812 (30TH)	47,752 (123,677)	4,523,628	Magnolia • Bald cypress • Eastern brown pelican

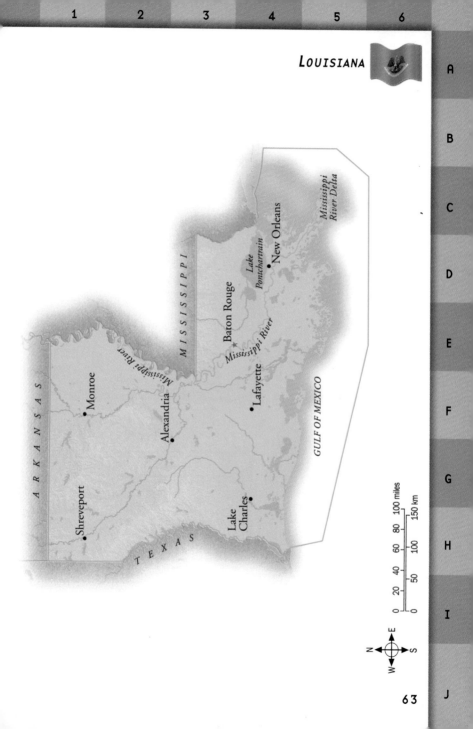

LOUISIANA

Mississippi

Mississippi

Mississippi's state capital is Jackson, on the Pearl River. However, the state itself takes its name from the great Mississippi River, which snakes down its western border. Over the ages the mud carried by the river has built up a long delta. The steamy climate is typical of the Gulf Coast. Near Natchez, one can still see grand homes that belonged to plantation owners in the 1800s. This cotton-growing state has more recently opened gambling casinos as a way of creating wealth.

▲ Cotton was key to Mississippi's economy in the 1800s and is still grown on many farms in the state.

DISCOVER MORE

"Mississippi" comes from *miisi-ziibi*, ("great river"), in the old language of the Ojibwe. The world's fourth-largest river system is the Mississippi–Missouri.

SEARCH AND FIND

★Jackson. F3	Hattiesburg G4
Biloxi. I5	Meridian. F5
Greenville. D2	Tupelo C5
Gulfport. I5	Vicksburg. F2

MISSISSIPPI FACTS

Statehood Date (Order)	Area sq mi (sq km)	Population	Flower • Tree • Bird
December 10, 1817 (20TH)	47,688 (123,516)	2,921,088	Magnolia • Magnolia • Mockingbird

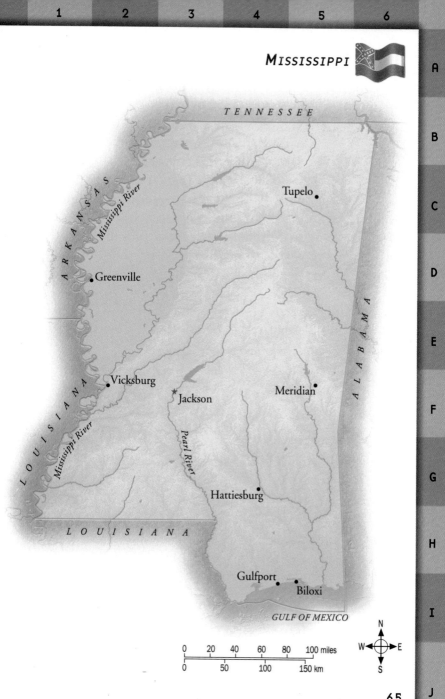

MISSISSIPPI

TENNESSEE

Tupelo

ARKANSAS

Mississippi River

Greenville

ALABAMA

Vicksburg

Jackson

Meridian

LOUISIANA

Mississippi River

Pearl River

Hattiesburg

LOUISIANA

Gulfport

Biloxi

GULF OF MEXICO

N
W ← ⊕ → E
S

| 0 | 20 | 40 | 60 | 80 | 100 miles |
| 0 | | 50 | | 100 | 150 km |

Appalachians

Alaska

United States

Hawaii

The southern Appalachian Mountains run northeast to southwest through Virginia, West Virginia, Tennessee, and North Carolina. They are the second-largest mountain range in America after the Rockies. Woodlands turn red and gold in the fall. The highlands drop to plateaus and coastal plains. Long sandy beaches, islands, and lagoons extend southward from the naval port of Norfolk, Virginia, down through the coast of South Carolina. The region is known for its coal mines and its racehorses. It also holds an important place in the history of American popular music, being the home of bluegrass, country music, and rock and roll.

SEARCH AND FIND

Kentucky	**Tennessee**
Frankfort D2	Nashville E2
North Carolina	**Virginia**
Raleigh E4	Richmond D4
South Carolina	**West Virginia**
Columbia F4	Charleston F4

REGION FACTS

	Highest elevation	Lowest elevation	State nickname	Major river(s)
Kentucky	Black Mountain 4,139 ft (1,262 m)	Mississippi River 257 ft (78 m)	Bluegrass State	Ohio, Tennessee, Cumberland
North Carolina	Mount Mitchell 6,684 ft (2,037 m)	Sea level	Old North State	Roanoke, Neuse, Cape Fear
South Carolina	Sassafras Mountain 3,560 ft (1,085 m)	Sea level	Palmetto State	Santee, Savannah, Saluda
Tennessee	Clingman's Dome 6,643 ft (2,025 m)	Mississippi River 178 ft (54 m)	Volunteer State	Mississippi, Tennessee
Virginia	Mount Rogers 5,729 ft (1,743 m)	Sea level	Old Dominion State	Potomac, James, Shenandoah
West Virginia	Spruce Knob 4,861 ft (1,481 m)	Potomac River 240 ft (73 m)	Mountain State	Potomac, Ohio, Kanawha

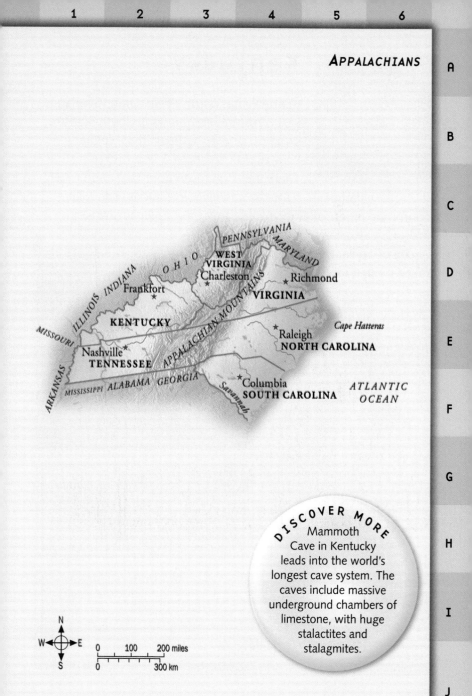

| 1 | 2 | 3 | 4 | 5 | 6 |

APPALACHIANS

A

B

C

D

PENNSYLVANIA

MARYLAND

OHIO

WEST
VIRGINIA

Charleston ★   ★ Richmond

Frankfort ★   VIRGINIA

ILLINOIS INDIANA

MISSOURI

KENTUCKY

APPALACHIAN MOUNTAINS

E

Cape Hatteras

★ Raleigh
NORTH CAROLINA

Nashville ★

TENNESSEE

ARKANSAS

MISSISSIPPI ALABAMA GEORGIA

Savannah

★ Columbia
SOUTH CAROLINA

*ATLANTIC
OCEAN*

F

G

H

I

J

DISCOVER MORE
Mammoth
Cave in Kentucky
leads into the world's
longest cave system. The
caves include massive
underground chambers of
limestone, with huge
stalactites and
stalagmites.

N
W ◄◆► E
S

0   100   200 miles
0   300 km

67

Kentucky

Kentucky

Kentucky lies south of the Ohio River and east of the Mississippi. In its southwest are swamps. In the southeast the Allegheny Plateau rises to about 3,000 ft (914 m). There are large reserves of coal and timber, and factories produce chemicals and electrical goods. The rolling countryside produces corn, wheat, fruit, and soybeans, while the bluegrass pastures around the city of Lexington are grazed by fine racehorses.

▶ *The Cumberland Gap is where pioneer Daniel Boone discovered a route through the Appalachian Mountains in 1775. It is now the nation's largest National Historic Park.*

DISCOVER MORE
The most famous horse race in the U.S.A. is the Kentucky Derby, run each year in Louisville since 1875. It is held on the first Saturday of May, and the crowds sing *My Old Kentucky Home*.

SEARCH AND FIND

★Frankfort	E2	Lexington	D3
Bowling Green	F4	Louisville	F2
Hopkinsville	G4	Owensboro	G3

KENTUCKY FACTS

Statehood Date (Order)	Area sq mi (sq km)	Population	Flower • Tree • Bird
June 1, 1792 (15TH)	40,410 (104,661)	4,173,405	Goldenrod • Kentucky coffee tree • Cardinal

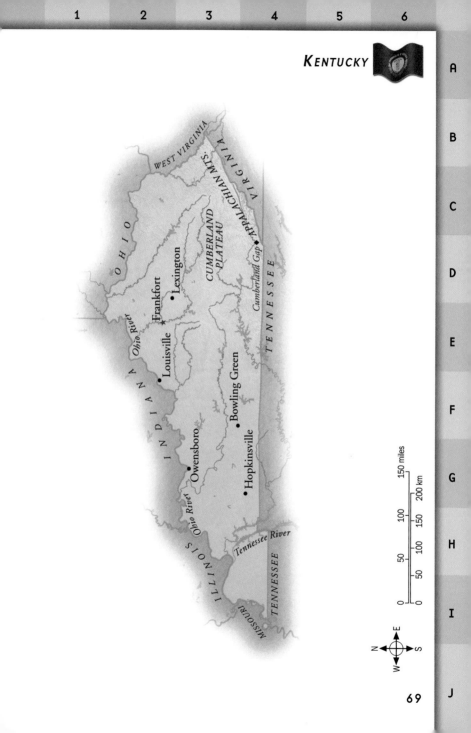

WEST VIRGINIA

OHIO

VIRGINIA

APPALACHIAN MTS.

CUMBERLAND PLATEAU

Cumberland Gap

Frankfort

Lexington

Ohio River

Louisville

INDIANA

TENNESSEE

Bowling Green

Owensboro

Hopkinsville

Ohio River

ILLINOIS

Tennessee River

TENNESSEE

MISSOURI

TENNESSEE

150 miles

200 km

100

150

100

50

50

0

0

N E S W

North Carolina

North Carolina

The Appalachian Mountains run down the border between North Carolina and Tennessee. To the east, the land drops to the rolling foothills of the Piedmont region, around the state capital, Raleigh. A plain forms a strip along the coast. The mainland shore is guarded from the open Atlantic Ocean by a long chain of grassy sandbars, called the Outer Banks. The climate is warm, and North Carolina's farms produce cotton, corn, soybeans, peanuts, and fruit. Charlotte is a center of banking, and the state also produces textiles, machinery, and the wooden furniture for which the state is famous.

▶ *The Blue Ridge Mountains are so called because of the blue tone that the forested slopes have from a distance.*

DISCOVER MORE
The lighthouse at Cape Hatteras is the tallest in the U.S.A. at 207 ft (63 m) high. In 1999, the whole structure had to be moved inland because the coastline was being eroded.

SEARCH AND FIND

★Raleigh	E3	Greensboro	F3
Charlotte	G3	Jacksonville	D4
Durham	E3	Wilmington	D4
Fayetteville	E3	Winston-Salem	F3

NORTH CAROLINA FACTS

Statehood Date (Order)	Area sq mi (sq km)	Population	Flower • Tree • Bird
November 21, 1789 (12TH)	52,669 (136,413)	8,683,242	Dogwood • Longleaf pine • Cardinal

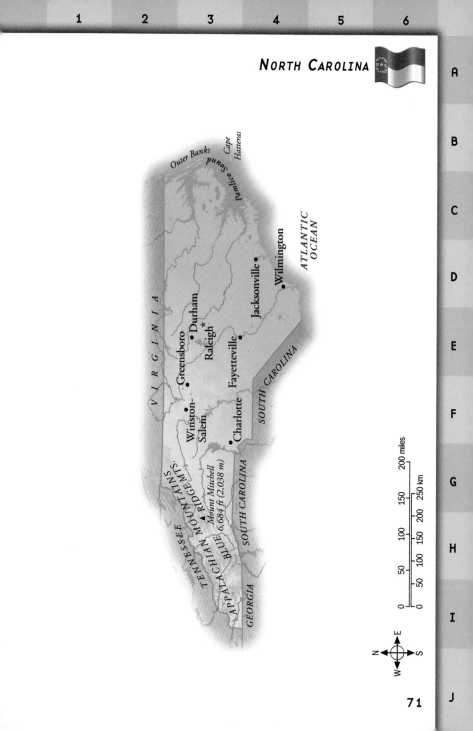

NORTH CAROLINA

Outer Banks
Cape Hatteras
Pamlico Sound

ATLANTIC OCEAN

Wilmington

Jacksonville

Durham
★ Raleigh
Greensboro

VIRGINIA

Fayetteville

Winston-Salem

Charlotte

SOUTH CAROLINA

TENNESSEE

APPALACHIAN MOUNTAINS
BLUE RIDGE MTS.
▲ Mount Mitchell
6,684 ft (2,038 m)

SOUTH CAROLINA

GEORGIA

200 miles

150   250 km
          200
100   150
50   100
          50
0   0

N
E
S
W

South Carolina

South Carolina

The beautiful old port of Charleston lies on the coast of South Carolina, a warm and humid state that borders the Savannah River. A tropical tree called palmetto thrives along the coast. Sea islands, sandy beaches, and salt marshes fringe a broad coastal plain. This area rises to the higher elevations of the Blue Ridge Mountains in the far northwest of the state, which form part of the Appalachian mountain chain. The state's traditional crop, cotton, gave rise to its textile and clothing industries.

▶ *Swamps are flooded wetland areas with trees and bushes. Many are found near the rivers in central South Carolina.*

DISCOVER MORE
A jazz dance that was popular with African Americans on the coast of South Carolina became a craze around the world in the 1920s. It is called the "Charleston."

SEARCH AND FIND

★Columbia. . . . .F3   Myrtle Beach . . .C3
Charleston. . . . .D4   Rock Hill. F1
Greenville. . . . . .G1   Spartanburg. . . .G1

SOUTH CAROLINA FACTS

Statehood Date (Order)	Area sq mi (sq km)	Population	Flower • Tree • Bird
May 23, 1788 (8TH)	31,113 (80,582)	4,255,083	Yellow jessamine • Palmetto • Great Carolina wren

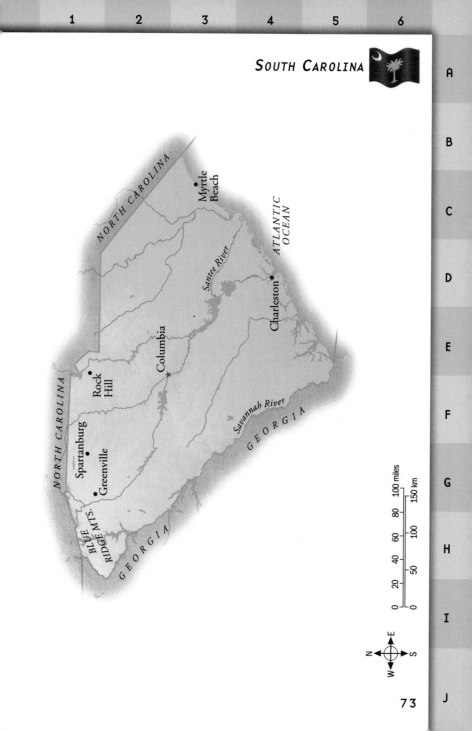

SOUTH CAROLINA

NORTH CAROLINA

Myrtle
Beach

ATLANTIC
OCEAN

Santee River

Charleston

Columbia

NORTH CAROLINA

Rock
Hill

Savannah River

GEORGIA

Sparranburg

Greenville

BLUE
RIDGE MTS.

GEORGIA

GEORGIA

100 miles	150 km
80	
60	100
40	50
20	
0	0

N E S W

Tennessee

Tennessee borders 8 other states.
It stretches from the east bank of the Mississippi River, with its port of Memphis, to the Great Smoky Mountains. These straddle the border with North Carolina. The state capital, Nashville, on the Cumberland River, is famous for being the center of country music. Half of the state is forested. In the other half, farms grow cotton and grain crops or raise cattle. Factories produce chemicals, fabrics, and electrical goods.

DISCOVER MORE
Tennessee is a great state if you are a turtle. It is home to 19 species and breeds including the stinkpot and the red-eared slider. Some box turtles live for more than 100 years.

SEARCH AND FIND

★Nashville. F3	Johnson City. . . .C3
Arlington I4	Kingsport. C3
Chattanooga. . . .E4	Knoxville D3
Clarksville G3	Memphis. I4
Jackson. H3	

▶ *Nashville is known as "Music City" and attracts musicians and music lovers from around the world.*

TENNESSEE FACTS

Statehood Date (Order)	Area sq mi (sq km)	Population	Flower • Tree • Bird
June 1, 1796 (16TH)	42,144 (109,152)	5,962,959	Bluebonnet • Pecan • Mockingbird

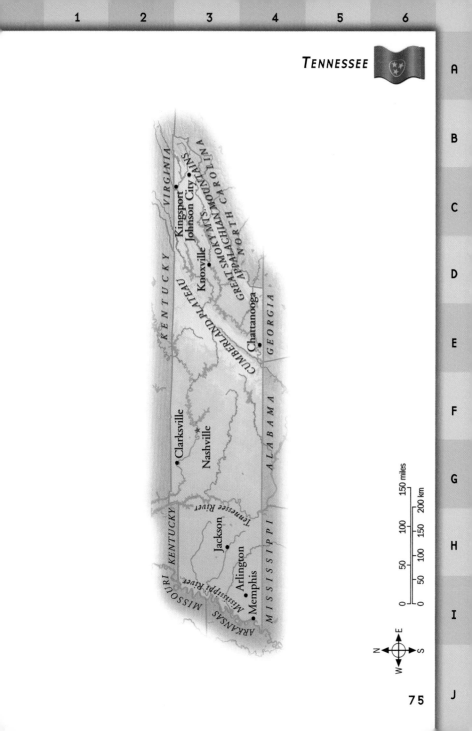

TENNESSEE

Virginia

Virginia

Western Virginia is known for the scenic Blue Ridge Mountains. Much of the state is rolling farmland, used for growing peanuts and tobacco, and raising cattle. The low-lying coastal area includes the marshy wilderness of the Great Dismal Swamp. Chesapeake Bay separates Virginia's Eastern Shore from the rest of the state. Most of the population lives in the cluster of cities around Richmond, Norfolk, and Virginia Beach. Industries include computing and communication technologies.

▼ *The city of Alexandria lies on the west bank of the Potomac River. Its historic center, shown here, is known as "Old Town" and was laid out in 1763.*

DISCOVER MORE
The Jamestown settlement dates back to 1607. It was the first successful British colony in North America. Today, you can see reconstructions of original buildings and ships.

SEARCH AND FIND

★Richmond	. . . .D3	Newport News	. .C4
Alexandria	. . . . .D2	Norfolk	. . . . . . .C4
Arlington	. . . . . .D2	Roanoke	. . . . . .F4
Jamestown	. . . .C3	Virginia Beach	. .C4
Lynchburg	. . . . .E3		

VIRGINIA FACTS

Statehood Date (Order)	Area sq mi (sq km)	Population	Flower • Tree • Bird
June 25, 1788 (10TH)	40,767 (105,586)	7,567,465	Dogwood • Dogwood • Cardinal

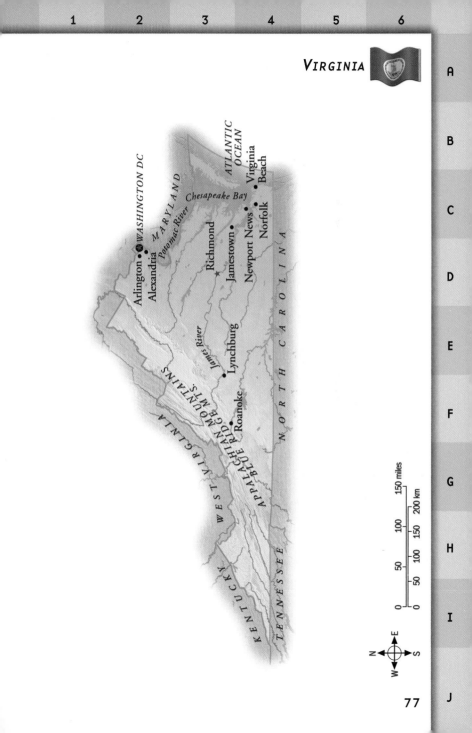

A

B

C

D

E

F

G

H

I

VIRGINIA

ATLANTIC OCEAN

Virginia Beach

Chesapeake Bay

Norfolk

WASHINGTON DC

MARYLAND

Potomac River

Richmond

Jamestown

Newport News

Arlington

Alexandria

NORTH CAROLINA

James River

Lynchburg

APPALACHIAN MTS.

BLUE RIDGE MTS.

Roanoke

WEST VIRGINIA

KENTUCKY

TENNESSEE

150 miles

200 km

100

150

100

50

50

0   0

N   E   S   W

J

West Virginia

West
Virginia

West Virginia lies on the banks of the Potomac and Ohio rivers. Most of the state is Appalachian Mountain country, and this includes the rocky Cumberland and Allegheny plateaus. The climate is cool for the region, with spruce forest on higher ground in the north. There are large reserves of mineral salt, coal, and timber, and cattle, sheep, and poultry are raised. Stained glasswork is an artistic tradition in the Ohio River Valley. West Virginia's two largest cities are Huntington, beside the Ohio River, and Charleston, the state capital.

▲ West Virginia is heavily forested and the trees produce blazing colors in the fall.

DISCOVER MORE
Nine species of bats live in Organ Cave, in the Greenbrier Valley. They include the northern big-eared bat, the Virginia big-eared bat, the silver-haired bat, and the small-footed bat.

SEARCH AND FIND

★Charleston	. . .G4	Morgantown.	. . .E2
Clarksburg	. . . . .F2	Parkersburg.	. . .G3
Huntington.	. . . .H4	Weirton	. . . . . . .F1
Martinsburg.	. . .C2	Wheeling	. . . . . .F2

WEST VIRGINIA FACTS

Statehood Date (Order)	Area sq mi (sq km)	Population	Flower • Tree • Bird
June 20, 1863 (35TH)	24,232 (62,760)	1,816,856	Rhododendron • Sugar maple • Cardinal

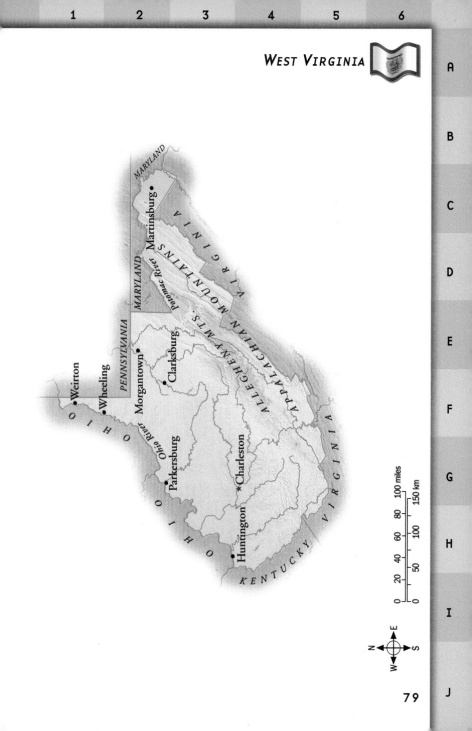

Alaska

United States

Hawaii

Southwest

Oil workers, farmers, and cattle ranchers are based in Oklahoma and Texas. The state of Texas is gigantic, stretching from the humid Gulf Coast to hot and dusty plains in the west. Houston, the largest city in Texas, is home to about 5 million people. The mountainous state of New Mexico and the deserts of Arizona border Mexico. Arizona's dizzying Grand Canyon is the world's largest gorge. It was carved out of the rock by the Colorado River for a length of 247 mi (349 km).

◀ *The saguaro cactus is found chiefly in southern Arizona and can grow up to 50 ft (15 m) in height.*

SEARCH AND FIND

Arizona	**Oklahoma**
Phoenix D1	Oklahoma City . . C5
New Mexico	**Texas**
Santa Fe C3	Austin E5

REGION FACTS

	Highest elevation	Lowest elevation	State nickname	Major river(s)
Arizona	Humphreys Peak 12,633 ft (3,851 m)	Colorado River 70 ft (21m)	Centennial State	Colorado, Gila, Little Colorado
New Mexico	Wheeler Peak 13,161 ft (4,011 m)	Red Bluff Reservoir 2,842 ft (846 m)	Sunshine State	Rio Grande, Pecos, Gila
Oklahoma	Black Mesa 4,973 ft (1,515 m)	Little River 289 ft (88m)	Sooner State	Arkansas, Red, Canadian
Texas	Guadelupe Peak 8,749 ft (2,667 m)	Sea level	Lone Star State	Rio Grande, Red, Pecos

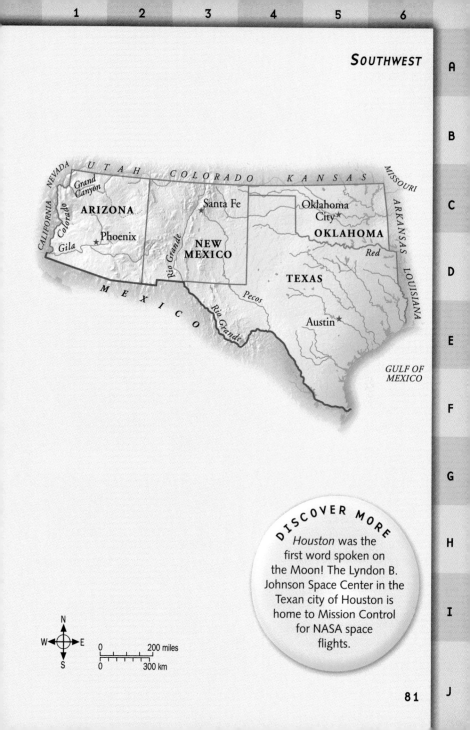

SOUTHWEST

NEVADA

UTAH   COLORADO   KANSAS   MISSOURI

Grand
Canyon

ARIZONA

Santa Fe ★

Oklahoma
City ★

OKLAHOMA

ARKANSAS

CALIFORNIA

Colorado

Phoenix ★

**NEW
MEXICO**

Rio Grande

Red

LOUISIANA

Gila

TEXAS

M E X I C O

Pecos

Rio Grande

Austin ★

*GULF OF
MEXICO*

N
W ← ✦ → E
S

0   200 miles
0   300 km

DISCOVER MORE

Houston was the
first word spoken on
the Moon! The Lyndon B.
Johnson Space Center in the
Texan city of Houston is
home to Mission Control
for NASA space
flights.

A

B

C

D

E

F

G

H

I

J

81

Arizona

The Colorado River has cut through the rocky plateau lands of northern Arizona, creating the long, deep gorge of the Grand Canyon. Erosion has created other spectacular landscapes, too, such as the dizzying 800-ft-high (244 m) pillars of Spider Rock. This is in Canyon de Chelly, in the homeland of the Navajo. Pine-clad highlands and sun-baked mountains drop to shimmering sandy deserts with tall cactus plants. Irrigation allows Arizona's farmers to grow cotton, fruit, and cereal crops. Important industries include oil and natural gas, telecommunications, and tourism. The largest city is the state capital, Phoenix.

▼ *Up to one mile (1.6 km) deep, the awesome Grand Canyon is famous for its sheer size and its colored rock formations.*

DISCOVER MORE
Where have trees turned to stone? In Arizona's Petrified Forest, great logs from the Triassic Period (between 200 and 250 million years ago) have survived as fossils in the rocks.

SEARCH AND FIND

★Phoenix......F3	Mesa.........F3
Flagstaff......D3	Tempe........F3
Glendale......F3	Tucson........G4
Lake Havasu City E1	Yuma.........G1

ARIZONA FACTS

Statehood Date (Order)	Area sq mi (sq km)	Population	Flower • Tree • Bird
February 14, 1912 (48TH)	114,000 (295,260)	5,939,292	Saguaro cactus blossom • Paloverde • Cactus wren

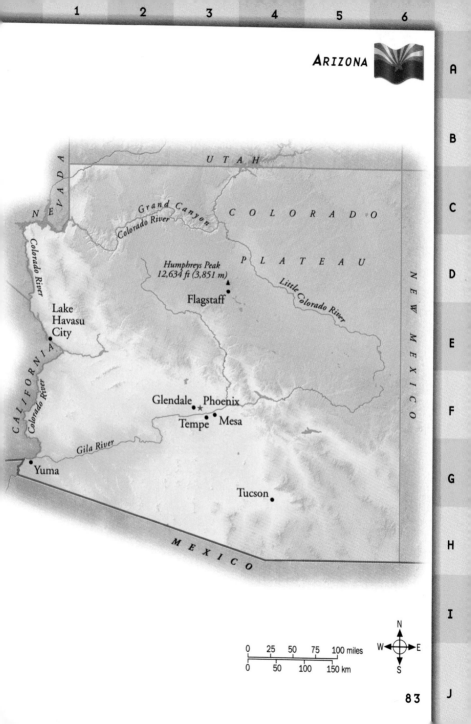

New Mexico

New Mexico

The Sangre de Cristo and San Juan mountains form the southern end of the mighty, snowcapped Rockies. These ranges drain into the Rio Grande, which flows through New Mexico's biggest city, Albuquerque. The river continues southward to form part of the U.S.–Mexico border. Southern New Mexico includes dusty pastures for cattle or sheep and deserts dotted with cacti, sagebrush, and yucca. Crops often need to be irrigated in this dry land, but farm produce includes pecan nuts, chili peppers, and feed for livestock. The state's economy also depends on the mining of uranium and potassium salts, and tourism.

DISCOVER MORE

At Skeleton Canyon, in the far southwest of New Mexico, a famous Native American Apache fighter named Geronimo surrendered to the U.S. cavalry in 1886.

▲ A common sight in New Mexico, the traditional chili ristras are strings of bright red chili peppers that are hung out to dry.

SEARCH AND FIND

★Santa Fe.....D3	Farmington.....C1
Albuquerque....E3	Las Cruces.....G3
Carlsbad......G5	Rio Rancho.....E3
Clovis.........E6	Roswell........F5

NEW MEXICO FACTS

Statehood Date (Order)	Area sq mi (sq km)	Population	Flower • Tree • Bird
January 6, 1912 (47TH)	121,593 (314,925)	1,928,384	Yucca flower • Pinion • Roadrunner

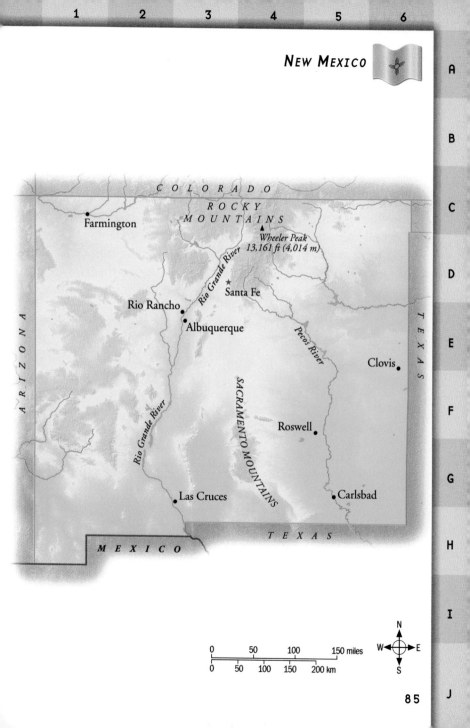

1   2   3   4   5   6

A

B

C

COLORADO

ROCKY
MOUNTAINS

Farmington

Wheeler Peak
13,161 ft (4,014 m)

D

Rio Grande River

Santa Fe

Rio Rancho

Albuquerque

Pecos River

E

A R I Z O N A

T E X A S

Clovis

F

Rio Grande River

SACRAMENTO MOUNTAINS

Roswell

G

Las Cruces

Carlsbad

H

M E X I C O

T E X A S

I

N
W   E
S

0   50   100   150 miles
0   50   100   150   200 km

J

Oklahoma

Oklahoma

Oklahoma lies on the southern edge of the Great Plains. A narrow strip of land reaches westward to the New Mexico state line. The Wichita and Arbuckle mountains rise from the southern plains, while the Ouachita and Boston mountains stretch eastward into Arkansas. This is a farming state, producing wheat, cotton, and cattle, but it is also a major center for oil, electronics, and telecommunications. Oklahoma City, in the center, is the lively state capital and a center for insurance, energy, and entertainment companies. Tulsa, in the northeast, employs people in oil, aerospace, and telecommunications industries.

▶ Tornadoes regularly occur in Oklahoma. These violent rotating columns of air can produce extremely high winds that can leave behind a trail of devastation.

DISCOVER MORE
Oklahoma has the largest Native American population of any state. More than 250,000 Native Americans live here. Many are descended from the original 67 tribes that inhabited the area.

SEARCH AND FIND

★Oklahoma City. E3	Norman. E3
Broken Arrow . . .C3	Stillwater. D3
Lawton. E4	Tulsa. D2

OKLAHOMA FACTS

Statehood Date (Order)	Area sq mi (sq km)	Population	Flower • Tree • Bird
November 16, 1907 (46TH)	69,956 (181,186)	3,547,884	Mistletoe • Redbud • Scissor-tailed flycatcher

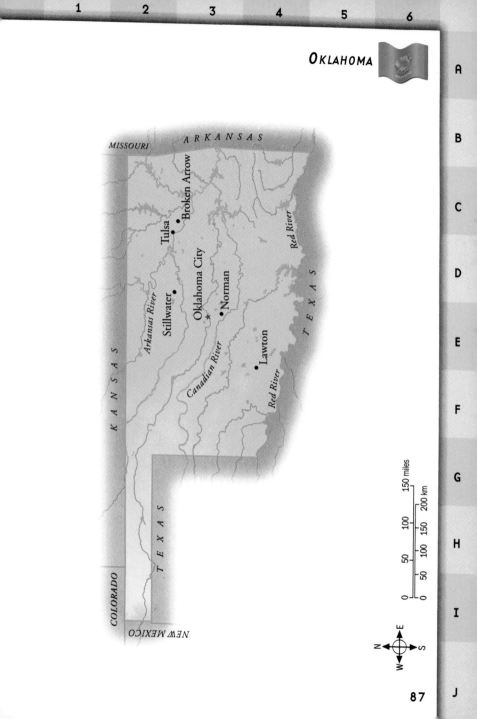

OKLAHOMA

MISSOURI

ARKANSAS

Broken Arrow

Tulsa

Red River

Oklahoma City

Norman

TEXAS

Arkansas River

Stillwater

KANSAS

Canadian River

Lawton

Red River

TEXAS

COLORADO

NEW MEXICO

150 miles

200 km

100

150

50

100

50

0

0

N
E
W
S

87

Texas

Texas

Texas is divided from Mexico by the Rio Grande River. It is the largest state after Alaska. From 1836 to 1845, Texas was an independent nation. Most of its rivers drain southeast into the Gulf of Mexico, which is fringed by islands and sandbars. Wide, hot plains stretch northward, while cooler mountains in the far west rise to 8,751 ft (2,667 m) at Guadalupe Peak. Texas is cowboy country, a land of cattle ranches where even business people may wear broad-brimmed Stetson hats. It is the chief oil producer in the U.S.A. This has brought great wealth to the state and to big cities such as Dallas and Houston.

▶ *These Texan cowboys demonstrate great skill with their lassoes while riding horseback.*

DISCOVER MORE

Six species of rattlesnake live in Texas. The longest and one of the heaviest is the Western Diamondback. The snake with the deadliest venom is the Mojave Rattlesnake.

SEARCH AND FIND

★Austin	.E4	Fort Worth	.D2
Amarillo	.G1	Galveston	.C4
Beaumont	.C4	Houston	.C4
Corpus Christi	.D5	Lubbock	.G2
Dallas	.D2	San Antonio	.E4
El Paso	.I3	Waco	.D3

TEXAS FACTS

Statehood Date (Order)	Area sq mi (sq km)	Population	Flower • Tree • Bird
December 29, 1845 (28TH)	266,808 (691,030)	22,859,968	Bluebonnet • Pecan • Mockingbird

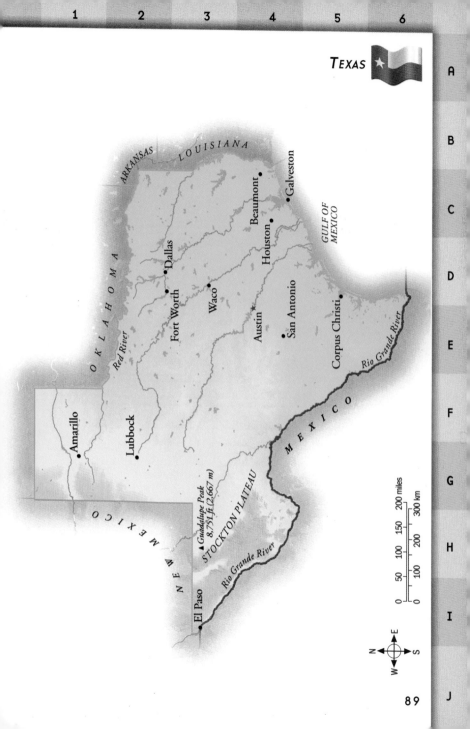

TEXAS

1	2	3	4	5	6

A

B

ARKANSAS
LOUISIANA

Galveston

Beaumont

C

GULF OF
MEXICO

Dallas

Houston

O K L A H O M A

D

Fort Worth

Waco

San Antonio

Red River

Austin

Corpus Christi

E

Rio Grande River

MEXICO

F

Amarillo

Lubbock

▲Guadalupe Peak
8,751 ft (2,667 m)

STOCKTON PLATEAU

G

200 miles

300 km

N E W   M E X I C O

150

H

Rio Grande River

100

200

50

100

El Paso

0

0

N E

N ⊕ S

W S

89

I

J

Midwest

Alaska

United States

Hawaii

The region between the Rocky Mountains and the upper Mississippi River is known as the Midwest. It includes the Great Plains, which are natural grasslands or prairies that are crossed by the mighty Missouri River.

The prairies are now farmed for wheat, corn, and soybeans. They form a vast patchwork of fields across the states of Missouri, Kansas, Iowa, and Nebraska. Fewer people live in the cattle country of North and South Dakota. The state of Minnesota, located beside Lake Superior, has dairy farms and reserves of iron ore.

SEARCH AND FIND

Iowa
Des Moines E4
Kansas
Topeka F4
Minnesota
St. Paul C4
Missouri
Jefferson City . . .F5

Nebraska
Lincoln E3
North Dakota
Bismarck C2
South Dakota
Pierre D2

REGION FACTS

	Highest elevation	Lowest elevation	State nickname	Major river(s)
Iowa	Hawkeye Point 1,670 ft (509 m)	Mississippi River 480 ft (146 m)	Hawkeye State or Corneye State	Mississippi, Des Moines
Kansas	Mount Sunflower 4,039 ft (1,231 m)	Verdigris River 679 ft (207 m)	Sunflower State	Missouri, Kansas, Arkansas
Minnesota	Eagle Mountain 2,301 ft (701 m)	Lake Superior 602 ft (183 m)	North Star State or Gopher State	Minnesota, St. Croix, Mississippi
Missouri	Taum Sauk Mountain 1,772 ft (540 m)	St. Francis River 230 ft (70 m)	Show Me State	Missouri, Grand, Mississippi
Nebraska	Johnson Township 5,424 ft (1,653 m)	Missouri River 840 ft (256 m)	Cornhusker State or Beef State	Missouri, Platte, Republican
North Dakota	White Butte 3,506 ft (1,068 m)	Red River 750 ft (229 m)	Flickertail State or Sioux State	Red, Missouri, James
South Dakota	Harney Peak 7,242 ft (2,207 m)	Big Stone Lake 966 ft (294 m)	Mount Rushmore State	James, Missouri, Cheyenne

CANADA

GREAT PLAINS

MONTANA

NORTH DAKOTA

Bismarck ★

Missouri

SOUTH DAKOTA

Pierre ★

Missouri

WYOMING

NEBRASKA

Platte

Republican

Lincoln ★

COLORADO

KANSAS

Kansas

Topeka ★

OKLAHOMA

MINNESOTA

Mississippi

Minnesota

St. Paul ★

WISCONSIN

Lake Superior

IOWA

Des Moines ★

• Davenport

Mississippi

ILLINOIS

Jefferson City ★

MISSOURI

Mississippi

ARKANSAS

N W E S

| 0 | 100 | 200 miles |
| 0 | 100 | 200 | 300 km |

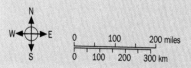

DISCOVER MORE
For a century or more the cougar, a wild big cat, has supposedly been extinct in the Midwest. New reports suggest it is now returning to Midwest farmland from the wilder parts of North America.

Iowa

Iowa

Iowa's green countryside is mostly flat and open, lying on the eastern section of the Great Plains between the Mississippi and Missouri rivers. The climate is hot and humid in the summer, and often snowy in the winter. Iowa is still chiefly a farming state, growing corn and soybeans, or raising cattle and hogs. Its factories process foods and manufacture farm machinery and household electrical goods. The city of Des Moines is a center for insurance companies.

▶ The state capitol building in Des Moines, built in 1886, has 30 different types of marble used in its construction.

DISCOVER MORE
Along the valley of the Mississippi River lie some strange bumps, some shaped like bears or birds. These mounds, made by Native American peoples, mark ancient burial sites.

SEARCH AND FIND

★Des Moines. . .F4	Fort Dodge. F3
Cedar Rapids. . .D3	Iowa City D4
Council Bluffs. . .H4	Sioux City I3
Davenport C4	Waterloo E3

IOWA FACTS

Statehood Date (Order)	Area sq mi (sq km)	Population	Flower • Tree • Bird
December 28, 1846 (29TH)	56,275 (145,753)	2,966,334	Wild rose • Oak • Eastern goldfinch

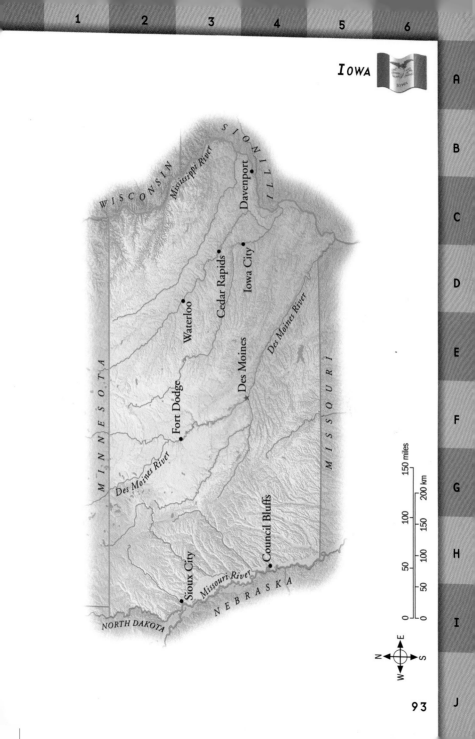

IOWA

1 2 3 4 5 6

A B C D E F G H I J

WISCONSIN
ILLINOIS
Mississippi River
Davenport
Cedar Rapids
Iowa City
Waterloo
Des Moines
Des Moines River
Fort Dodge
MINNESOTA
MISSOURI
Des Moines River
Council Bluffs
Sioux City
Missouri River
NEBRASKA
NORTH DAKOTA

150 miles
200 km
100
150
50
100
50
0
0

N E S W

93

Kansas

Kansas is at the geographical center of the continental United States. Rolling lowlands are crossed by the Missouri, Kansas, and Arkansas rivers. The prairies were once rolling grasslands, but today are farmed for wheat. That is why Kansas is sometimes called a "breadbasket" state. Its farms also grow corn, sorghum, and soybeans, and raise cattle. Many industries in Kansas are also linked with farming, such as flour mills, grain factories, and meatpacking. The land rises to a height of 4,135 ft (1,260 m) in the west. The biggest city in Kansas, Wichita, is home to firms that make small aircraft and executive jets.

▲ *Kansas is one of the leading producers of wheat in the U.S.A.—its soil is very fertile. Harvesters are a common sight.*

DISCOVER MORE

Tourists visiting Dodge City take a trip back to the 1870s. Located on the old Santa Fe Trail, Dodge City was one of the most famous cowboy towns in North America.

SEARCH AND FIND

★Topeka C3	Kansas City. . . .B3
Dodge City. G4	Lawrence. C3
Hutchison. E4	Salina E3
Junction City. . . .D3	Wichita. E4

KANSAS FACTS

Statehood Date (Order)	Area sq mi (sq km)	Population	Flower • Tree • Bird
January 29, 1861 (34TH)	82,277 (213,098)	2,744,687	Sunflower • Cottonwood • Western meadowlark

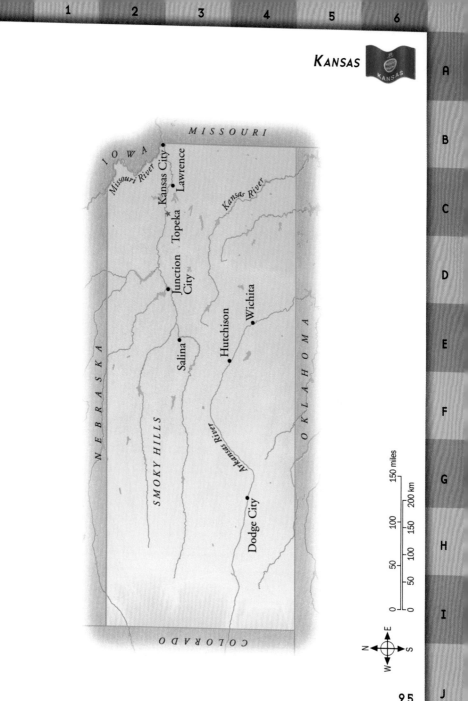

KANSAS

Minnesota

Minnesota

Minnesota is the largest state in the Midwest. Glacier movement in prehistoric times gouged out thousands of lakes across the state. The Mississippi River rises in the north. Timber and iron are still produced in this region, and at Hibbing is the world's biggest opencast iron ore mine, a hole in the ground on a massive scale. Prairie lands are farmed for corn, soybeans, and sugar beets. Ships carry cargoes from the lakeside port of Duluth to the Atlantic Ocean. The "Twin Cities" of Minneapolis and St. Paul are home to about 3 million people.

▶ *Known as the "Land of 10,000 lakes," Minnesota also has more than 69,000 mi (111,000 km) of natural rivers and streams.*

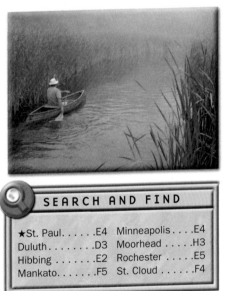

DISCOVER MORE
In 1979, Scott and Brennan Olson from Minneapolis designed the Rollerblade, a new form of the roller skate. It was the first "in-line" skate that could be used for fast sports.

SEARCH AND FIND

★St. Paul	E4	Minneapolis	E4
Duluth	D3	Moorhead	H3
Hibbing	E2	Rochester	E5
Mankato	F5	St. Cloud	F4

MINNESOTA FACTS

Statehood Date (Order)	Area sq mi (sq km)	Population	Flower • Tree • Bird
May 11, 1858 (32ND)	75,385 (218,601)	5,132,799	Pink and white lady's slipper • Red pine • Loon

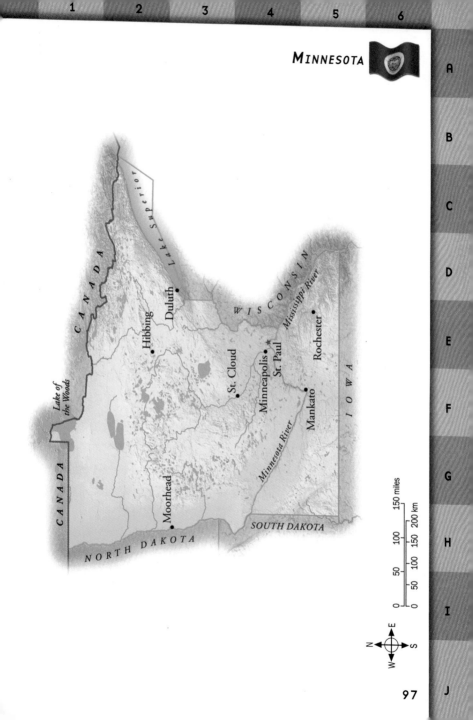

MINNESOTA

A
B
C
D
E
F
G
H
I
J

1 2 3 4 5 6

CANADA

Lake Superior

Duluth

Hibbing

Lake of
the Woods

CANADA

St. Cloud

Minneapolis
St. Paul

Minnesota River

Moorhead

NORTH DAKOTA

SOUTH DAKOTA

WISCONSIN

Mississippi River

Rochester

Mankato

IOWA

150 miles
100
50
0

200 km
150
100
50
0

N
E
S
W

97

Missouri

Missouri

Missouri takes its name from the great river that flows across the state. Missouri means "river of the big canoe" in the Algonquin language. Low-lying prairies rise to the Ozark Mountains on the Arkansas border. Farmers grow soybeans and grains, and breed cattle and hogs. Missouri's mineral resources include lead and limestone. St. Louis has long been regarded as the gateway to the west, because in the 19th century it was the starting point for many wagons heading westward across the Great Plains. The Gateway Arch, a huge arc of steel towering over the city, was raised in 1965 as a memorial to westward expansion.

▲ The Gateway Arch rises to 630 ft (192 m) high on the St. Louis skyline.

DISCOVER MORE
Hannibal was the boyhood home of writer Samuel Langhorne Clemens (1835–1910) who wrote under the name of "Mark Twain." He invented the famous character Huckleberry Finn.

SEARCH AND FIND

★Jefferson City.	.E3	Kansas City	.G3
Cape Girardeau..	C4	Springfield	.F4
Columbia	E2	St. Joseph	.H2
Hannibal	E2	St. Louis	.D3

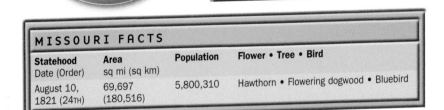

MISSOURI FACTS

Statehood Date (Order)	Area sq mi (sq km)	Population	Flower • Tree • Bird
August 10, 1821 (24TH)	69,697 (180,516)	5,800,310	Hawthorn • Flowering dogwood • Bluebird

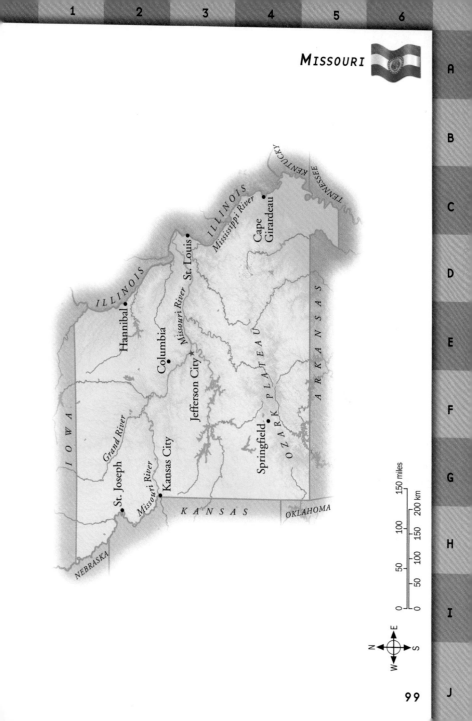

MISSOURI

Nebraska

Nebraska

Nebraska occupies the west bank of the muddy Missouri River. A wide, open stretch of prairie under a big sky, it is planted with grain and vegetable crops or is used to raise beef cattle. The land is drained by the Platte River system. In the western part of the state, toward Wyoming, sit sandy hills and eroded rocks. These were useful landmarks for the pioneers, whose covered wagons rolled westward in the mid-19th century. Omaha is Nebraska's biggest city, a center of telecommunications, banking, and food-based industries.

▶ *Chimney Rock in western Nebraska served as a landmark to westward-bound pioneers in the 1800s.*

DISCOVER MORE
During the Miocene Epoch, 20 million years ago, rhinoceroses were common in Nebraska. Their remains have been found at the Agate Fossil Beds National Monument.

SEARCH AND FIND

★Lincoln	C4	Norfolk	D3
Grand Island	E4	North Platte	G4
Hastings	E4	Omaha	C3

NEBRASKA FACTS

Statehood Date (Order)	Area sq mi (sq km)	Population	Flower • Tree • Bird
March 1, 1867 (37TH)	77,355 (200,350)	1,758,787	Goldenrod • Cottonwood • Western meadowlark

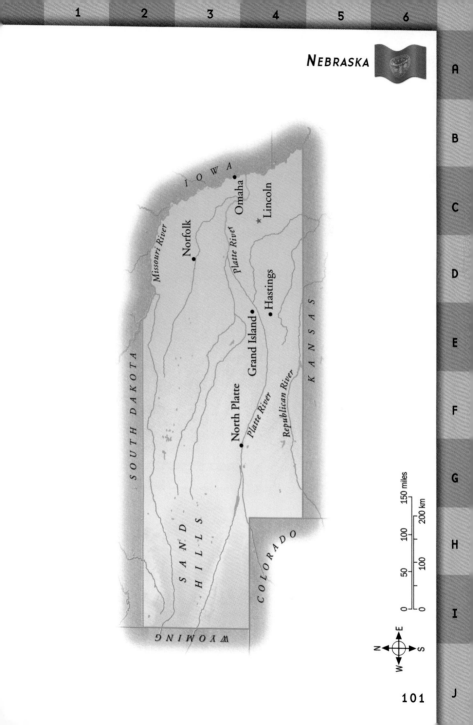

NEBRASKA

North Dakota

North Dakota's rolling grasslands are farmed for wheat, barley, flax, soybeans, and sunflowers. Most of the state's population lives in the east, where the small cities of Fargo and Grand Forks occupy the Red River valley. The state is divided in two by the Missouri River. In the western part of the state, the rim of the Great Plains rises to mountains and plateau lands whose rocks have been shaped by wind and water.

▶ North Dakota is the leading producer of sunflowers in the U.S.A. They are grown for their oil and their seeds.

DISCOVER MORE
North Dakota is visited each fall by millions of snow geese. The birds fly from the Arctic to Mexico, in flocks of up to 1,000. Their flight rises and falls, so they are called "wavies."

SEARCH AND FIND

★Bismarck F4	Grand Forks C3
Dickinson H4	Minot G2
Fargo B4	Williston I2

NORTH DAKOTA FACTS

Statehood Date (Order)	Area sq mi (sq km)	Population	Flower • Tree • Bird
November 2, 1889 (39TH)	70,702 (183,119)	636,677	Prairie rose • American elm • Western meadowlark

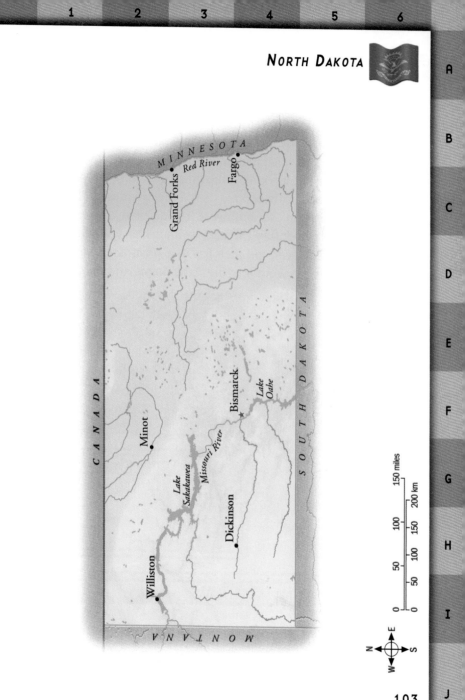

NORTH DAKOTA

MINNESOTA

Grand Forks

Red River

Fargo

CANADA

SOUTH DAKOTA

Bismarck

Lake Oahe

Minot

Lake Sakakawea

Missouri River

Dickinson

Williston

MONTANA

150 miles

200 km

100

150

50

100

50

0

0

N
W   E
S

South Dakota

South Dakota

South Dakota is a prairie state, growing wheat, oats, and corn. Rainfall drains into the Cheyenne, White, and James rivers, which join up in their turn with the mighty Missouri. Cattle graze on shortgrass pastures. The processing of foodstuffs and meats is a major industry. The gold-rich Black Hills rise in the southwest. The desolate, barren, rocky Badlands were named because the early settlers believed they were good for nothing. However, this area has its own strange beauty and the rocks have been worn into dramatic points and gorges.

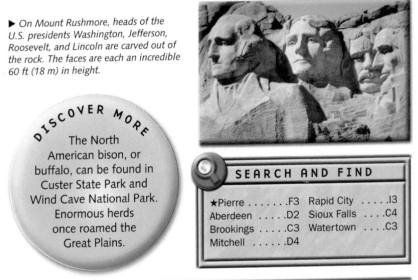

▶ *On Mount Rushmore, heads of the U.S. presidents Washington, Jefferson, Roosevelt, and Lincoln are carved out of the rock. The faces are each an incredible 60 ft (18 m) in height.*

DISCOVER MORE
The North American bison, or buffalo, can be found in Custer State Park and Wind Cave National Park. Enormous herds once roamed the Great Plains.

SEARCH AND FIND

★Pierre F3	Rapid City I3
Aberdeen D2	Sioux Falls C4
Brookings C3	Watertown C3
Mitchell D4	

SOUTH DAKOTA FACTS

Statehood Date (Order)	Area sq mi (sq km)	Population	Flower • Tree • Bird
November 2, 1889 (40TH)	77,116 (199,730)	775,933	Pasque flower • Black Hills spruce • Ring-necked pheasant

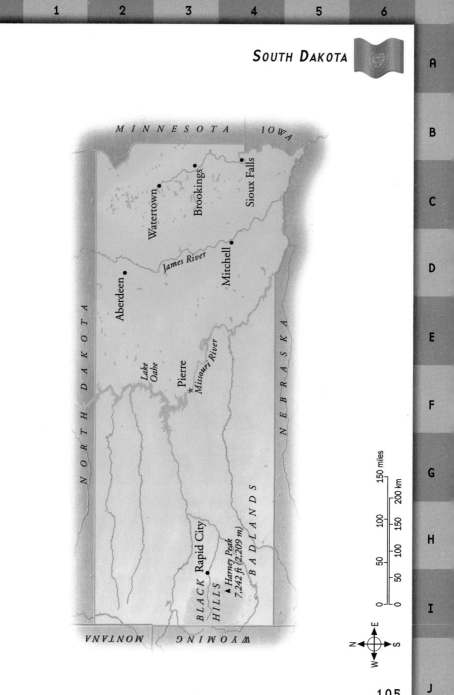

MINNESOTA   IOWA

Sioux Falls

Brookings

Watertown

James River

Mitchell

Aberdeen

NORTH DAKOTA

Lake Oahe

Pierre

Missouri River

NEBRASKA

BADLANDS

Rapid City

BLACK HILLS

▲ Harney Peak
7,242 ft (2,209 m)

WYOMING   MONTANA

150 miles

200 km

100
150

50
100

50

0
0

N
E
W
S

Great Lakes

The states that make up the Great Lakes region lie on the Canadian border. They are fringed by dunes, rocks, and forests. Several large cities are situated on their shores, including Cleveland, Ohio, and Chicago, Illinois, with its famous skyscrapers. Michigan is a well known center of the automobile industry. Wisconsin's farms support dairy farming, while wheat, soybeans, and corn are grown in Ohio, Michigan, Illinois, and Indiana.

SEARCH AND FIND

Illinois
Springfield G2

Indiana
Indianapolis . . .F4

Michigan
Lansing E4

Ohio
Columbus. F5

Wisconsin
Madison. E2

DISCOVER MORE

Indianapolis stages the "Indy 500," the best-known motor race in the U.S.A. The speedway, nicknamed "the Brickyard," has a 2.5 mi (4 km) circuit. The race is 500 mi (805 km) long.

REGION FACTS

	Highest elevation	Lowest elevation	State nickname	Major river(s)
Illinois	Charles Mound 1,235 ft (376 m)	Mississippi 279 ft (85m)	Prairie State	Mississippi, Illinois, Ohio
Indiana	Hoosier Hill 1,257 ft (383 m)	Wabash River 320 ft (98 m)	Hoosier State	Wabash, Ohio, White
Michigan	Mount Arvon 1,979 ft (603 m)	Lake Erie 572 ft (174m)	Wolverine State or Great Lakes State	Grand, Muskegon, Kalamazoo
Ohio	Campbell Hill 1,549 ft (472 m)	Ohio River 455 ft (139m)	Buckeye State	Ohio, Scioto, Miami
Wisconsin	Timms Hill 1,951 ft (595 m)	Lake Michigan 581 ft (177 m)	Badger State	Mississippi, Saint Croix, Wisconsin

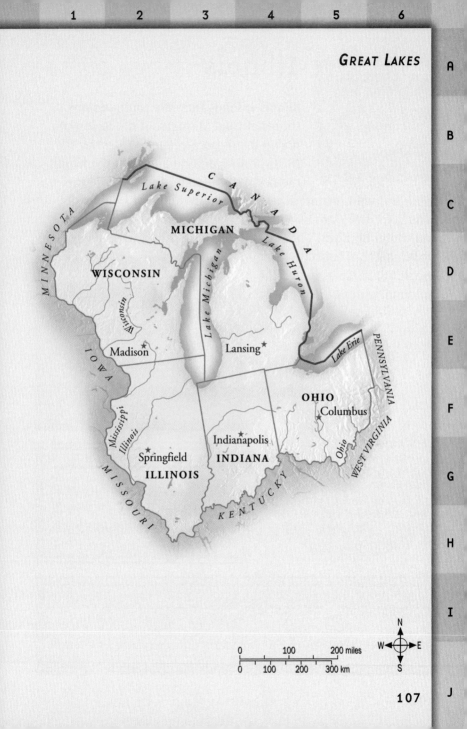

Illinois

Illinois

Illinois extends from the southwestern shores of Lake Michigan. It is a region of prairie that is bordered in the west by the Mississippi River. Corn is grown chiefly in the north of the state, and wheat in the south and west. Illinois experiences a wide range of weather conditions, from storms and high winds to summer heat waves and winter blizzards. The state's biggest city is Chicago, a major world center of business, finance, and trading. More than 9 million people live in Chicago and the surrounding area.

▶ *Illinois' economy thrives on a mix of industry and agriculture, and farms large and small can be found across the state.*

DISCOVER MORE
The Sears Tower skyscraper in Chicago was built in 1973. It is currently the tallest building in North America. The radio mast on the top reaches a height of 1,729 ft (527 m).

SEARCH AND FIND

★Springfield. . . .E3	Decatur E4
Aurora C4	East St. Louis . .G2
Bloomington. . . .D4	Peoria D3
Champaign. E5	Rockford B4
Chicago. C5	

ILLINOIS FACTS

Statehood Date (Order)	Area sq mi (sq km)	Population	Flower • Tree • Bird
December 3, 1818 (21st)	56,345 (145,934)	12,763,371	Violet • White oak • Cardinal

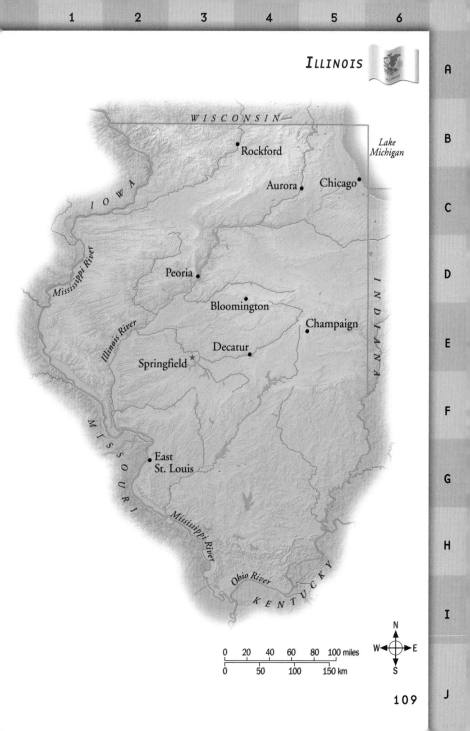

ILLINOIS

Indiana

People from Indiana are known as Hoosiers.
Nobody quite knows why, although there
are many different explanations. Indiana lies
between the Ohio River and the southern
tip of Lake Michigan. Summers are hot, but
winters are long and chilly. The state is crossed by the Wabash
River. Broad, level farmland, once forested, produces corn, winter
wheat, soybeans, melons, and tomatoes.
Poultry is raised here, too. Indianapolis,
the state capital, is famous as a center
of amateur sports. Indiana has
limestone and rich coalfields. Its
factories and mills make steel,
chemicals, medicines, machinery,
and automobiles.

DISCOVER MORE
One town in
southern Indiana is
named Santa Claus.
Originally founded by
German immigrants, it
was given its festive
name on Christmas
Eve, 1852.

▲ Soybeans, shown here being harvested,
are a major cash crop in the state.

SEARCH AND FIND

★Indianapolis . .F4	Muncie E5
Bloomington . . .G3	Santa Claus . . .H2
Evansville I1	South Bend B3
Fort Wayne C5	Terre Haute F1
Gary B1	

INDIANA FACTS

Statehood Date (Order)	Area sq mi (sq km)	Population	Flower • Tree • Bird
December 11, 1816 (19TH)	36,185 (93,720)	6,271,973	Peony • Tulip tree • Cardinal

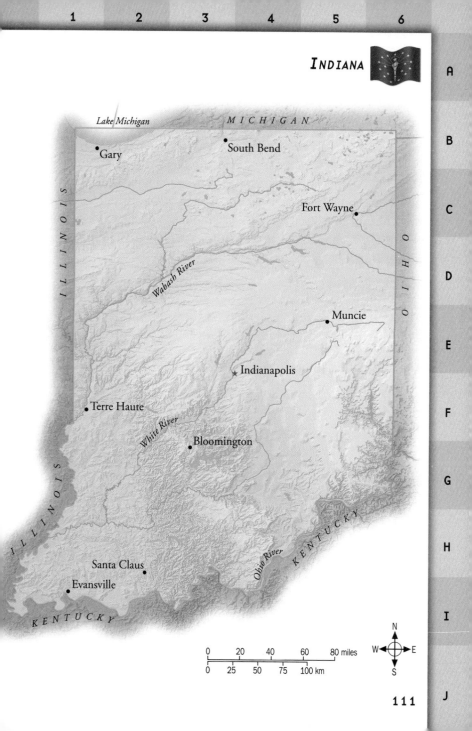

INDIANA

1 2 3 4 5 6

A
B
C
D
E
F
G
H
I
J

Lake Michigan

MICHIGAN

Gary
South Bend

Fort Wayne

ILLINOIS

Wabash River

OHIO

Muncie

★ Indianapolis

Terre Haute

White River

Bloomington

ILLINOIS

KENTUCKY

Santa Claus

Ohio River

KENTUCKY

Evansville

KENTUCKY

N
W   E
S

0   20   40   60   80 miles
0   25   50   75   100 km

Michigan

Michigan

Michigan is made up of two enormous peninsulas that extend into the Great Lakes, bordering Canada. They are linked by the Mackinac Bridge. The long Upper Peninsula is a land of forests and highlands with a small population. The Lower Peninsula, shaped like a mitten, points north. The city of Detroit, as well as Grand Rapids, Dearborn, and Flint, are major centers of the U.S. automobile industry. Rural areas produce sugar beets, potatoes, and grains.

▲ *The buildings of downtown Detroit are situated along the Detroit River. Just across the river lies the town of Windsor, Ontario, in Canada.*

DISCOVER MORE

Dr. Will Keith Kellogg accidentally invented cornflakes in Battle Creek, Michigan, in 1894, while he was experimenting with vegetarian recipes.

SEARCH AND FIND

★Lansing	.G5	Flint	.F5
Ann Arbor	.G5	Grand Rapids	.F4
Battle Creek	.G4	Kalamazoo	.G4
Bay City	.F5	Marquette	.D2
Detroit	.G6	Saginaw	.F5

MICHIGAN FACTS

Statehood Date (Order)	Area sq mi (sq km)	Population	Flower • Tree • Bird
January 26, 1837 (26TH)	58,527 (151,586)	10,120,860	Apple blossom • White pine • Robin

MICHIGAN

Lake Superior

CANADA

WISCONSIN

Upper Peninsula

• Marquette

Lake Michigan

Lake Huron

Lower

Peninsula

Bay City •
• Saginaw
Grand
Rapids • • Flint
Lansing ★
Battle Creek • Detroit •
Kalamazoo • Ann Arbor •
CANADA

INDIANA OHIO Lake Erie

0   50   100   150 miles

0   50 100 150   200 km

N
W ◀◆▶ E
S

Ohio

Ohio

Low-lying plains occupy the west of Ohio, while in the east, the Allegheny Plateau climbs to hills and forests. Farmers raise cattle and grow grain crops and soybeans. Ohio is a center for coal, steel, machinery, and rubber. These industries are based in the northern cities of Akron, Cleveland, and Toledo. Lake Erie provides routes for shipping. In the south, the Ohio River is used by the inland port of Cincinnati. Recently the state has moved toward service industries, such as finance and insurance.

▲ Cincinnati, on the Ohio River, hosts the largest annual gathering of steam riverboats in the country.

DISCOVER MORE
The term *rock 'n' roll* was first used in Ohio in 1951 by a disc jockey named Alan Freed. Today, Cleveland is the home of the Rock and Roll Hall of Fame.

SEARCH AND FIND

★Columbus	....F4	Cleveland	......D1
Akron	.........D2	Dayton	........H4
Canton	........D2	Toledo	........G1
Cincinnati	......H5	Youngstown	....C2

OHIO FACTS

Statehood Date (Order)	Area sq mi (sq km)	Population	Flower • Tree • Bird
March 1, 1803 (17TH)	41,330 (107,044)	11,464,042	Scarlet carnation • Buckeye • Cardinal

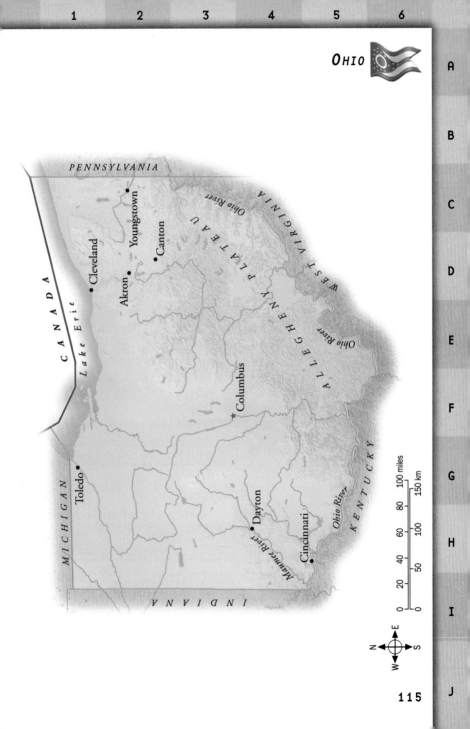

Ohio

| | 1 | 2 | 3 | 4 | 5 | 6 |

A

B

C — PENNSYLVANIA

Youngstown
Cleveland • Canton
Akron

CANADA

Lake Erie

WEST VIRGINIA

ALLEGHENY PLATEAU

Ohio River

Columbus ★

Toledo •

MICHIGAN

KENTUCKY

Dayton •
Cincinnati •

Maumee River

Ohio River

INDIANA

100 miles
150 km
80 — 100
60 —
40 — 50
20 —
0 — 0

N
W — E
S

J

Wisconsin

Wisconsin

Wisconsin is a state brimming with lakes and rivers. The rolling, green countryside meets flat prairie lands in the southwest. Wisconsin's rich pastures are grazed by dairy cattle, and the state is known for its milk and cheese. Large forests provide timber. The lakeside port of Milwaukee is the state's largest city. Breweries made Milwaukee famous, but today, it is better known as one of the U.S.A.'s major centers of manufacturing. It is also important for its financial services.

▶ *Dairy farming is one of Wisconsin's leading industries—and the state is known as "America's Dairyland." These Holstein cattle live on a farm in southern Wisconsin.*

DISCOVER MORE
Wisconsin's waterways are home to the beaver—the biggest rodent in North America. The heaviest Wisconsin beaver on record weighed 110 lb (50 kg).

SEARCH AND FIND

★Madison	.....E5	La Crosse	.....G4
Appleton	......D4	Milwaukee	.....D5
Eau Claire	.....G3	Oshkosh	......D4
Green Bay	.....D3	Sheboygan	.....D4
Kenosha	......D5	Superior	.......H1

WISCONSIN FACTS

Statehood Date (Order)	Area sq mi (sq km)	Population	Flower • Tree • Bird
May 29, 1848 (30TH)	56,153 (145,436)	5,536,201	Wood violet • Sugar maple • Robin

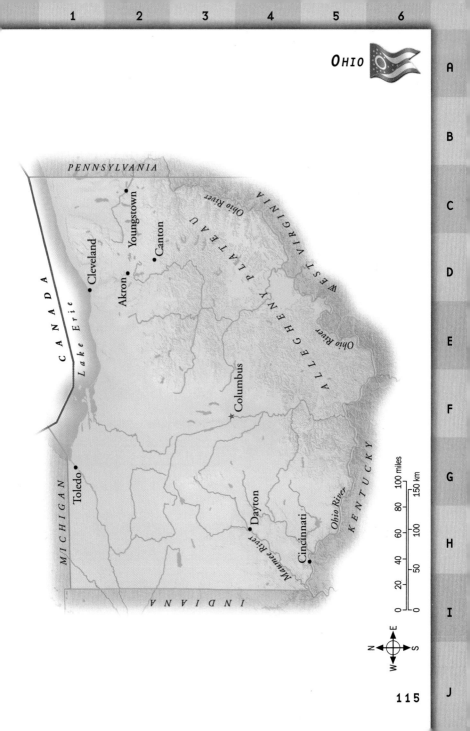

Ohio

Wisconsin

Wisconsin

Wisconsin is a state brimming with lakes and rivers. The rolling, green countryside meets flat prairie lands in the southwest. Wisconsin's rich pastures are grazed by dairy cattle, and the state is known for its milk and cheese. Large forests provide timber. The lakeside port of Milwaukee is the state's largest city. Breweries made Milwaukee famous, but today, it is better known as one of the U.S.A.'s major centers of manufacturing. It is also important for its financial services.

▶ *Dairy farming is one of Wisconsin's leading industries—and the state is known as "America's Dairyland." These Holstein cattle live on a farm in southern Wisconsin.*

DISCOVER MORE
Wisconsin's waterways are home to the beaver—the biggest rodent in North America. The heaviest Wisconsin beaver on record weighed 110 lb (50 kg).

SEARCH AND FIND

★Madison	.....E5	La Crosse	.....G4
Appleton	......D4	Milwaukee	.....D5
Eau Claire	.....G3	Oshkosh	......D4
Green Bay	.....D3	Sheboygan.	.....D4
Kenosha	......D5	Superior.	......H1

WISCONSIN FACTS

Statehood Date (Order)	Area sq mi (sq km)	Population	Flower • Tree • Bird
May 29, 1848 (30TH)	56,153 (145,436)	5,536,201	Wood violet • Sugar maple • Robin

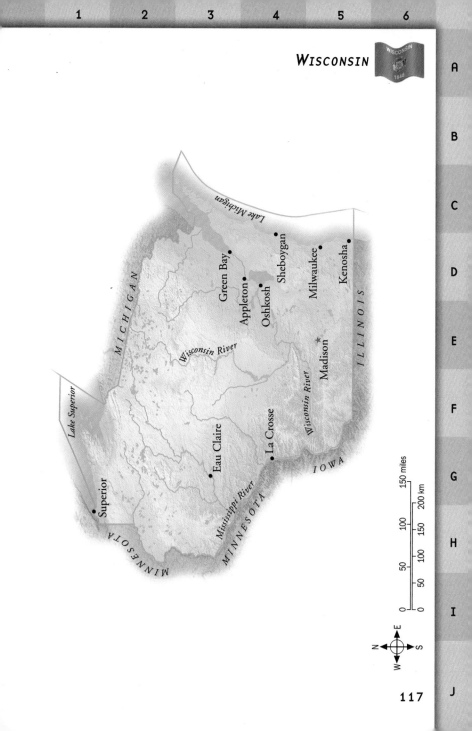

WISCONSIN

1 2 3 4 5 6

A
B
C
D
E
F
G
H
I
J

Lake Michigan

MICHIGAN

Green Bay
Appleton
Oshkosh
Sheboygan
Milwaukee
Kenosha

ILLINOIS

Wisconsin River

Madison

Wisconsin River

Lake Superior

Eau Claire

La Crosse

IOWA

Superior

Mississippi River

MINNESOTA

MINNESOTA

150 miles
200 km
100
150
100
50
50
0
0

N
E
S
W

117

Alaska

United States

Hawaii

Mountain

A series of rugged mountains forms the backbone of the North American continent. The Rocky Mountains rise to snowy summits, which tower over forests of pine and aspen. To the east, cattle are raised on the prairies of Montana and Wyoming. To the south, the peaks of Colorado attract skiers. West of the Rockies lie Idaho, Nevada, and Utah, with their striking landscapes of salt flats, canyons, and deserts in the Great Basin.

DISCOVER MORE
Yellowstone in Wyoming is the U.S.A.'s oldest national park, founded in 1870. It is full of hot springs, gurgling mud, and geysers. The most regular geyser, Old Faithful, gushes up to 180 ft (55 m).

SEARCH AND FIND

Colorado	**Nevada**
Denver G5	Carson City F1
Idaho	**Utah**
Boise E2	Salt Lake City F3
Montana	**Wyoming**
Helena D3	Cheyenne F5

REGION FACTS

	Highest elevation	Lowest elevation	State nickname	Major river(s)
Colorado	Mount Elbert 14,433 ft (4,399 m)	Arkansas River 3,350 ft (1,021 m)	Centennial State	Colorado, Arkansas, South Platte
Idaho	Borah Peak 12,662 ft (3,859 m)	Snake River 710 ft (216 m)	Gem State	Snake, Salmon, Kootenai
Montana	Granite Peak 12,799 ft (3,901 m)	Kootenai River 1,800 ft (549 m)	Treasure State	Missouri, Clark Fork, Yellowstone
Nevada	Boundary Peak 13,140 ft (4,005 m)	Beaverdam Peak 2,000 ft (610 m)	Silver State or Sagebrush State	Colorado, Humboldt, Columbia
Utah	Kings Peak 13,528 ft (4,123 m)	Beaverdam Wash 2,000 ft (610 m)	Beehive State	Colorado, Green, Sevier
Wyoming	Gannett Peak 13,804 ft (4,207 m)	Belle Fourche River 3,099 ft (945 m)	Equality State or Cowboy State	North Platte, Green, Bighorn

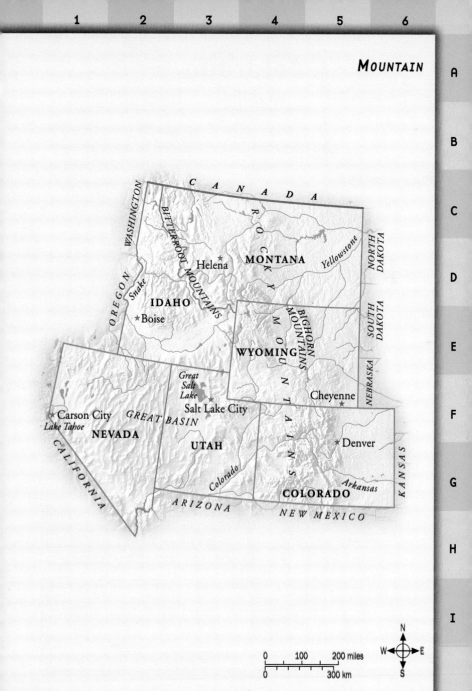

MOUNTAIN

CANADA

WASHINGTON

OREGON

ROCKY

BITTERROOT MOUNTAINS

Snake

MONTANA

Helena ★

Yellowstone

NORTH DAKOTA

IDAHO

★ Boise

SOUTH DAKOTA

BIGHORN MOUNTAINS

MOUNTAINS

WYOMING

NEBRASKA

Great Salt Lake

Salt Lake City ★

★ Carson City

GREAT BASIN

Lake Tahoe

NEVADA

Cheyenne ★

CALIFORNIA

UTAH

★ Denver

KANSAS

Colorado

Arkansas

ARIZONA

COLORADO

NEW MEXICO

N
W E
S

0   100   200 miles

0   300 km

Colorado

Colorado

Eastern Colorado is a land of rivers and prairies, set on the edge of the High Plains. The grasslands are grazed by cattle or sown with winter wheat. The region is dry, and water for crops generally has to be supplied by irrigation. In the western part of the state, the snowcapped peaks of the Rockies tower above forests of aspen and pine. The tallest mountain, Mount Elbert, is 14,433 ft (4,399 m) high. Winter sports, such as skiing and snowboarding, and other outdoor activities attract tourists. Denver, the state capital, has many government offices and firms working in energy, communications, and the mining of gold, silver, uranium, gypsum, and coal.

▶ *These houses at Mesa Verde National Park in southwestern Colorado were built hundreds of years ago by Pueblo peoples.*

DISCOVER MORE
Colorado is the mountain giant of the U.S.A. No fewer than 54 of its summits top 14,000 ft (4,267 m). That helps to make it the state with the highest average altitude.

SEARCH AND FIND

★Denver E3	Fort Collins. E2
Boulder E2	Grand Junction . .H3
Colorado	Greeley D2
Springs. E3	Pueblo. D4

COLORADO FACTS

Statehood Date (Order)	Area sq mi (sq km)	Population	Flower • Tree • Bird
August 1, 1876 (38TH)	104,091 (269,596)	4,665,177	Rocky Mountain columbine • Colorado blue spruce • Prairie lark-finch

COLORADO

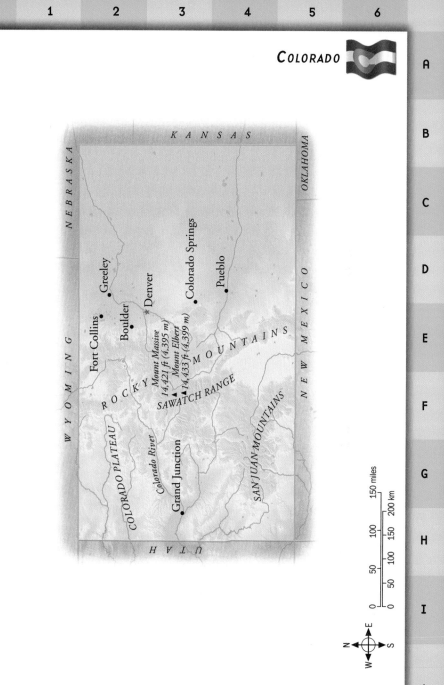

KANSAS

NEBRASKA

OKLAHOMA

Greeley

Colorado Springs

Denver

Pueblo

Fort Collins

Boulder

WYOMING

NEW MEXICO

Mount Massive
14,421 ft (4,395 m)

Mount Elbert
14,433 ft (4,399 m)

R O C K Y   M O U N T A I N S

SAWATCH RANGE

COLORADO PLATEAU

Colorado River

Grand Junction

SAN JUAN MOUNTAINS

U T A H

150 miles

100

50

0

200 km

150

100

50

0

N E S W

A
B
C
D
E
F
G
H
I
J

Idaho

Idaho

The Bitterroot Range, part of the Rocky Mountains, rises along the state border between Idaho and Montana. The Salmon River Mountains form a central highland region between the rushing white waters of the Snake and Salmon rivers. Much of Idaho is remote wilderness, attracting adventurous hikers, rafters, and fishers. Areas that can be farmed, often with the help of irrigation, produce wheat and the potatoes for which the state is famous. The state capital, Boise, lies in the southwest. It has developed high-tech industries such as electronics and computing.

▲ The mighty Snake River, 1,038 mi (1,670 km) in length, winds through much of southern Idaho.

DISCOVER MORE
An unusual landscape to the north of the Snake River Plain is the "Craters of the Moon." Made up of black cones, cinders, craters, and lava flows, it was created by volcanic activity.

SEARCH AND FIND

★Boise . . . . . . G1   Nampa G1
Coeur d'Allene . .C1   Pocatello. H5
Idaho Falls. . . . .G5   Twin Falls. H3
Lewiston D1

IDAHO FACTS

Statehood Date (Order)	Area sq mi (sq km)	Population	Flower • Tree • Bird
July 3, 1890 (43RD)	83,564 (216,423)	1,429,096	Syringa • White pine • Mountain bluebird

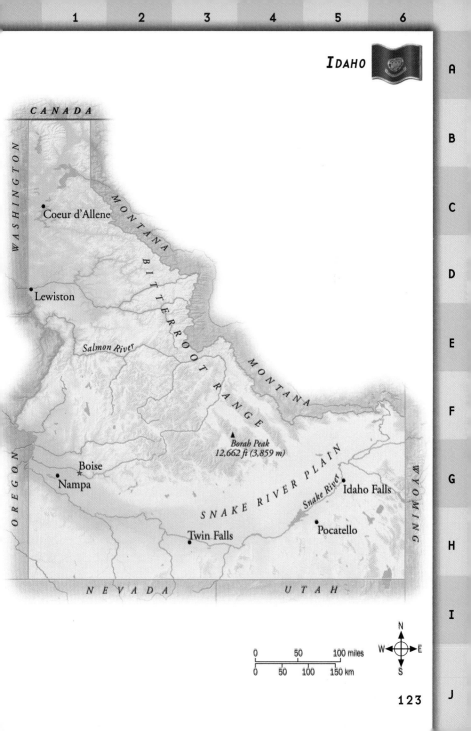

IDAHO

CANADA

WASHINGTON

Coeur d'Allene

MONTANA

BITTERROOT RANGE

Lewiston

Salmon River

MONTANA

▲ Borah Peak
12,662 ft (3,859 m)

Boise ★
Nampa

SNAKE RIVER PLAIN

Snake River

Idaho Falls

WYOMING

Twin Falls

Pocatello

OREGON

NEVADA

UTAH

N
W ◄ ✦ ► E
S

| 0 | 50 | 100 miles |
| 0 | 50 | 100 | 150 km |

Montana

Montana

Montana is one of the Rocky Mountain states. Its highest summits are in the west and south, reaching 12,799 ft (3,904 m) at Granite Peak. In the east, the mountains descend to the Yellowstone River and the Great Plains. Winters are cold and snowy, and summers are warm. Montana is thinly populated, apart from towns such as Helena, Great Falls, and Billings. Forests, rivers, cattle ranches, and fields of wheat and barley make up the landscape. Resources include oil and gas, coal, gold, silver, and copper.

▶ *Agriculture is the greatest source of income in the U.S.A., and enormous wheat fields are a common sight in Montana.*

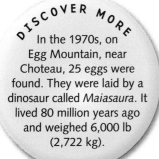

DISCOVER MORE
In the 1970s, on Egg Mountain, near Choteau, 25 eggs were found. They were laid by a dinosaur called *Maiasaura*. It lived 80 million years ago and weighed 6,000 lb (2,722 kg).

SEARCH AND FIND

★Helena	.G3	Choteau	.G3
Billings	.E4	Great Falls	.F3
Bozeman	.F4	Kalispell	.H2
Butte	.G4	Missoula	.H3

MONTANA FACTS

Statehood Date (Order)	Area sq mi (sq km)	Population	Flower • Tree • Bird
November 8, 1889 (41ST)	147,046 (380,848)	935,670	Bitterroot • Ponderosa pine • Western meadowlark

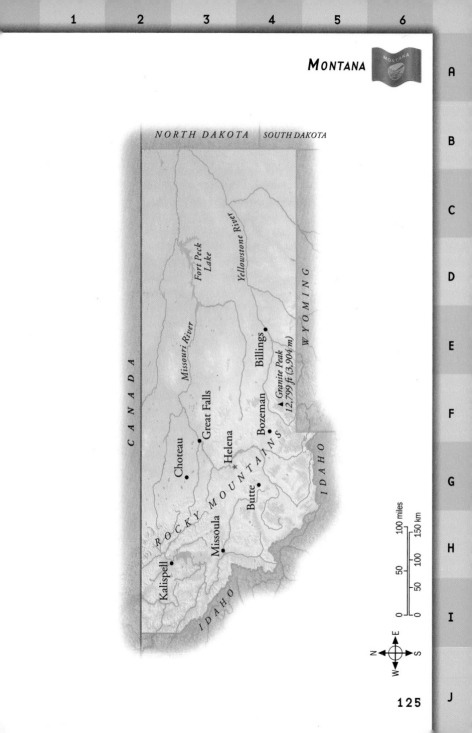

MONTANA

Nevada

Nevada

Nevada lies in the Great Basin region, between California and Utah. This is a very dry region of desert and sagebrush, eroded rocks, canyons, and snow-streaked mountains. Water must be very carefully managed to support any farming or towns. In this harsh landscape, there are cities such as Reno, Carson City, and glittering Las Vegas, which is famous for entertainment on a lavish scale. Gaming is a major industry in Nevada, along with tourism, the manufacturing of electrical goods, and the mining of silver, gold, and gypsum.

▶ *The Hoover Dam on the Colorado River forms a huge concrete arch standing an impressive 221 m (726 ft) high.*

DISCOVER MORE
Rodents called kangaroo rats thrive in Nevada's deserts, even though there are no pools of water to drink. Their bodies can convert even the driest seeds they eat into liquid.

SEARCH AND FIND

★Carson City . . .E1   Las Vegas H5
Elko . . . . .C4   Reno D1
Henderson H5

NEVADA FACTS

Statehood Date (Order)	Area sq mi (sq km)	Population	Flower • Tree • Bird
October 31, 1864 (36TH)	110,561 (286,352)	2,414,807	Sagebrush • Single leaf pinon • Mountain bluebird

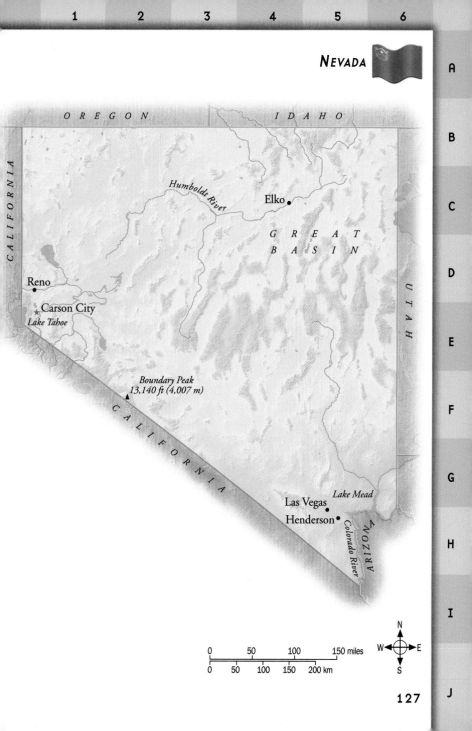

NEVADA

OREGON

IDAHO

CALIFORNIA

Humboldt River

Elko •

GREAT

BASIN

Reno •

Carson City
★
Lake Tahoe

UTAH

Boundary Peak
13,140 ft (4,007 m)
▲

CALIFORNIA

Lake Mead

Las Vegas
•
Henderson •

Colorado River

ARIZONA

| 0 | 50 | 100 | 150 miles |

| 0 | 50 | 100 | 150 | 200 km |

N
W ◆ E
S

Utah

Utah

In Utah, the Rocky Mountains climb to 13,572 ft (4,123 m) at Kings Peak. The Rockies' western slopes descend to the Great Basin region. Here, rivers and lakes evaporate to form shimmering flats of white mineral salts. Every world land speed record since 1935 has been achieved on the Bonneville Salt Flats or in the Black Rock Desert. Canyons, buttes, and natural arches of pink and brown sandstone have been formed by the Colorado River, attracting many tourists. To the west of the Wasatch Mountains are Utah's chief population centers. The biggest is Salt Lake City, founded by people of the Mormon faith.

▲ *Bryce Canyon in southwestern Utah is known for its striking rock formations.*

DISCOVER MORE
The first railroad to cross the U.S.A. was built from east and west simultaneously. The two railroads (Central Pacific and Union Pacific) were joined at Promontory on May 10, 1869.

SEARCH AND FIND

★Salt Lake City	.D3	Promontory	.C2
Brigham City	.C3	Provo	.D3
Cedar City	.G1	St. George	.H1
Ogden	.C3	West Valley City	.D3
Orem	.D3		

UTAH FACTS

Statehood Date (Order)	Area sq mi (sq km)	Population	Flower • Tree • Bird
January 4, 1896 (45TH)	84,899 (219,889)	2,469,585	Sego lily • Blue spruce • American seagull

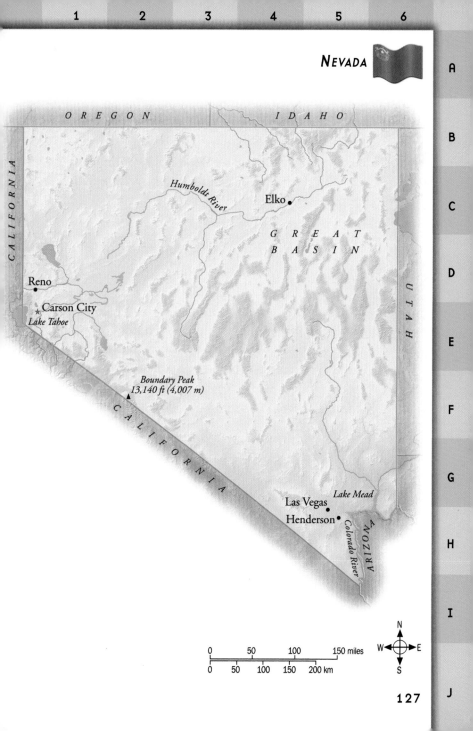

NEVADA

A

B

OREGON   IDAHO

Humboldt River   Elko •

C

CALIFORNIA

G R E A T
B A S I N

D

Reno
•
Carson City
★
Lake Tahoe

U T A H

E

Boundary Peak
13,140 ft (4,007 m)
▲

C
A
L
I
F
O
R
N
I
A

F

G

Las Vegas
•
Henderson •

Lake Mead

Colorado River

A
R
I
Z
O
N
A

H

I

0   50   100   150 miles
0   50   100   150   200 km

N
W ◆ E
S

J

Utah

Utah

In Utah, the Rocky Mountains climb to 13,572 ft (4,123 m) at Kings Peak. The Rockies' western slopes descend to the Great Basin region. Here, rivers and lakes evaporate to form shimmering flats of white mineral salts. Every world land speed record since 1935 has been achieved on the Bonneville Salt Flats or in the Black Rock Desert. Canyons, buttes, and natural arches of pink and brown sandstone have been formed by the Colorado River, attracting many tourists. To the west of the Wasatch Mountains are Utah's chief population centers. The biggest is Salt Lake City, founded by people of the Mormon faith.

▲ *Bryce Canyon in southwestern Utah is known for its striking rock formations.*

DISCOVER MORE
The first railroad to cross the U.S.A. was built from east and west simultaneously. The two railroads (Central Pacific and Union Pacific) were joined at Promontory on May 10, 1869.

SEARCH AND FIND

★Salt Lake City .D3   Promontory C2
Brigham City. . . .C3   Provo. D3
Cedar City . . . . .G1   St. George. H1
Ogden . . . . .C3   West Valley City .D3
Orem. D3

UTAH FACTS

Statehood Date (Order)	Area sq mi (sq km)	Population	Flower • Tree • Bird
January 4, 1896 (45TH)	84,899 (219,889)	2,469,585	Sego lily • Blue spruce • American seagull

1   2   3   4   5   6

A

B

C

D

E

F

G

H

I

J

IDAHO

Promontory • Brigham City

Great
Salt Lake

Ogden

G r e a t
S a l t
L a k e
D e s e r t

Salt Lake City
★
West Valley City

Black Rock
Desert

Orem

Provo

WYOMING

▲
Kings Peak
13,572 ft (4,123 m)

Bonneville
Salt Flats

N E V A D A

C O L O R A D O

WASATCH RANGE

Colorado River

Cedar City •

Lake
Powell

St. George
•

C O L O R A D O   P L A T E A U

ARIZONA

0   25   50   75   100 miles

0   50   100   150 km

N
W ⬥ E
S

Wyoming

Wyoming

Wyoming has low rainfall, so farmers tend to raise cattle rather than grow crops that need a lot of water. The state capital, Cheyenne, plays host to rodeos that display traditional ranching and cowboy skills. A series of majestic, rugged mountain ranges, such as the Bighorn and the Teton, form a broad section of the Rockies. The slopes descend to plateaus, which are bordered in the east by the prairie lands of the Great Plains. With a population of little more than 509,000, Wyoming has the lowest population of any state. Industries include coal mining and tourism, which is based around national parks such as Grand Teton and Yellowstone.

DISCOVER MORE
The town of Cody is named after William "Buffalo Bill" Cody (1846–1915), a famous "Wild West" figure. He worked for the Pony Express, and was a soldier, a buffalo hunter, and a showman.

▼ American Bison graze amid spectacular mountain scenery in Grand Teton National Park in western Wyoming.

SEARCH AND FIND

★Cheyenne	. . . .D5	Green River	. . . .G4
Casper	. . . . . . .E3	Laramie	. . . . . . .D5
Cody	. . . . .G2	Rock Springs	. . .G4
Gillette	. . . . . . .D2	Sheridan	. . . . . .E2

WYOMING FACTS

Statehood Date (Order)	Area sq mi (sq km)	Population	Flower • Tree • Bird
July 10, 1890 (48TH)	97,809 (253,326)	509,294	Indian paintbrush • Cottonwood • Western meadowlark

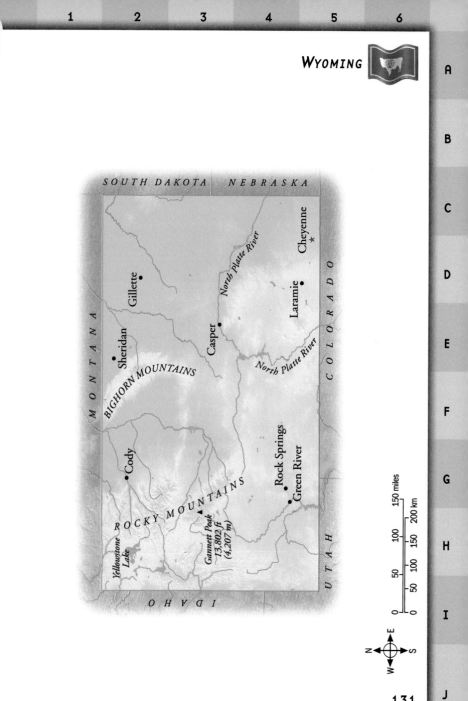

WYOMING

1 2 3 4 5 6

A B C D E F G H I J

SOUTH DAKOTA   NEBRASKA

Cheyenne ★

North Platte River

MONTANA

Gillette •

Sheridan •

BIGHORN MOUNTAINS

Casper •

Laramie •

COLORADO

North Platte River

Cody •

Rock Springs •
Green River •

ROCKY MOUNTAINS

▲ Gannett Peak
13,802 ft
(4,207 m)

Yellowstone Lake

UTAH

IDAHO

150 miles
100   200 km
150
50   100
50
0   0

N
W   E
S

West Coast

Alaska

United States

Hawaii

The Sierra Nevada, Coast, and Cascade mountain ranges run parallel to the rocky Pacific coast. Ocean winds bring rainfall to their western slopes. The Californian climate is warm in the south and cool in the north. Fruit crops are grown in irrigated valleys. Major cities include Los Angeles, a world center for the entertainment industries, and San Francisco, perched above a wide, blue bay. Northward, through Oregon to Washington, are misty forests and volcanic peaks. The chief port of the north is Seattle, Washington.

SEARCH AND FIND

California	Washington
Sacramento F3	Olympia C3
Oregon	
Salem. C3	

DISCOVER MORE
One of the most destructive volcanic eruptions in U.S. history happened in Washington State in 1980. The summit of Mount Saint Helens was blasted 15 mi (24 km) into the sky.

▼ The famous Golden Gate Bridge has a total span of 1.7 mi (2.7 km) across San Francisco Bay.

REGION FACTS

	Highest elevation	Lowest elevation	State nickname	Major river(s)
California	Mount Whitney 14,494 ft (4,478m)	Death Valley −282 ft (−86m)	Golden State	Sacramento, San Joaquin, Colorado
Oregon	Mount Hood 11,239 ft (3,426 m)	Sea level	Beaver State	Columbia, John Day, Snake
Washington	Mount Rainier 14,410 ft (4,392 m)	Sea level	Evergreen State	Columbia, Snake, Yakima

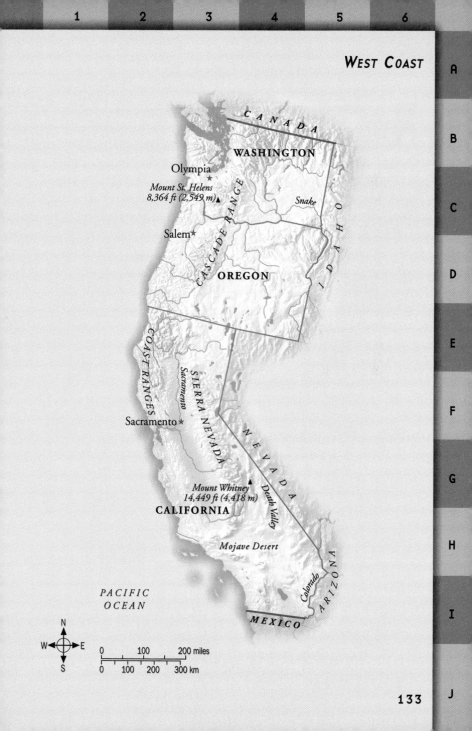

CANADA

WASHINGTON

Olympia ★
Mount St. Helens
8,364 ft (2,549 m) ▲

Snake

IDAHO

CASCADE RANGE

Salem ★

OREGON

COAST RANGES

SIERRA NEVADA

Sacramento

Sacramento ★

NEVADA

Mount Whitney
14,449 ft (4,418 m) ▲

Death Valley

CALIFORNIA

Mojave Desert

Colorado

ARIZONA

PACIFIC
OCEAN

MEXICO

N
W ◆ E
S

0   100   200 miles
0   100   200   300 km

California

California

Pine trees and hills border California's shoreline, which rises to the Coast Ranges. The valleys of the Sacramento and San Joaquin rivers run down the center of the state, and the high, snowy peaks of the Sierra Nevada form a barrier in the east. Climate varies greatly, from the fierce, dry heat of southern deserts to cool, misty forests in the north. Irrigation helps farmers to grow citrus fruits, vegetables, and grapes. The city and surrounds of Los Angeles are home to nearly 13 million people. Farther north is the bay-side city of San Francisco. The southern Bay area is nicknamed Silicon Valley because of the huge quantitites of silicon chips produced there. These chips powered the personal computer revolution in the 1980s and 90s.

▲ The Hollywood suburb of Los Angeles is famous worldwide for its movies.

SEARCH AND FIND

★Sacramento. . .E2   Oxnard G3
Bakersfield . . . .G3   Riverside. G4
Fresno . . . . .F3   San Diego H4
Los Angeles. . . .G4   San Francisco. . .E1
Modesto . . . . . .E2   San Jose. E2

DISCOVER MORE
A Californian record-breaking tree is a sequoia called "General Sherman." It is the world's most massive tree, 275 ft (83.8 m) high and 102 ft (31.3 m) around the trunk.

CALIFORNIA FACTS

Statehood Date (Order)	Area sq mi (sq km)	Population	Flower • Tree • Bird
September 9, 1850 (31ST)	158,707 (411,049)	36,132,147	Golden poppy • California redwood • California valley quail

CALIFORNIA

A

B

C

D

OREGON

NEVADA

Sacramento River

★ Sacramento

San Francisco •

• Modesto

San Jose •

SIERRA NEVADA

White Mountain Peak
▲ *14,246 ft (4,342 m)*

NEVADA

E

San Joaquin River

• Fresno

▲ *Mount
Whitney
14,449 ft
(4,418 m)*

Death Valley

F

*PACIFIC
OCEAN*

C O A S T   R A N G E S

• Bakersfield

Mojave Desert

G

• Oxnard

Los Angeles •

• Riverside

ARIZONA

H

San Diego •

MEXICO

I

N
W ✛ E
S

0   50   100   150   200 miles

0   100   200   300 km

J

Oregon

Oregon

Oregon is a state with very large forests. These have supplied the papermaking and construction industries with timber, but the need for conservation in recent years has reduced the number of trees being cut down. Much of the state is mountainous. Its ranges descend to the fertile valley of the Willamette River, site of the state's largest city, Portland, which is famous for its roses. The valley also produces fruit, nuts, wine, and dairy products. Oregon's Great Sandy Desert in the southeast rises to the Blue Mountains in the northeast. The great Columbia River, on its westward course from the Rockies to the Pacific Ocean, forms the border with Washington State.

DISCOVER MORE
Cannon Beach, on Oregon's coast, has a Sandcastle Day. Sea lions, bears, dinosaurs, mermaids, and even castles are sculpted from sand—only to be washed away by the next tide.

SEARCH AND FIND

★Salem H2	Medford H5
Bend F3	Portland H2
Corvallis H3	Roseburg H4
Eugene H3	Woodburn. H2

▶ Oregon's Crater Lake was formed when a crater collapsed at the summit of an extinct volcano in the Cascade Range.

OREGON FACTS

Statehood Date (Order)	Area sq mi (sq km)	Population	Flower • Tree • Bird
February 14, 1859 (33RD)	97,073 (251,419)	3,641,056	Oregon grape • Douglas fir • Western meadowlark

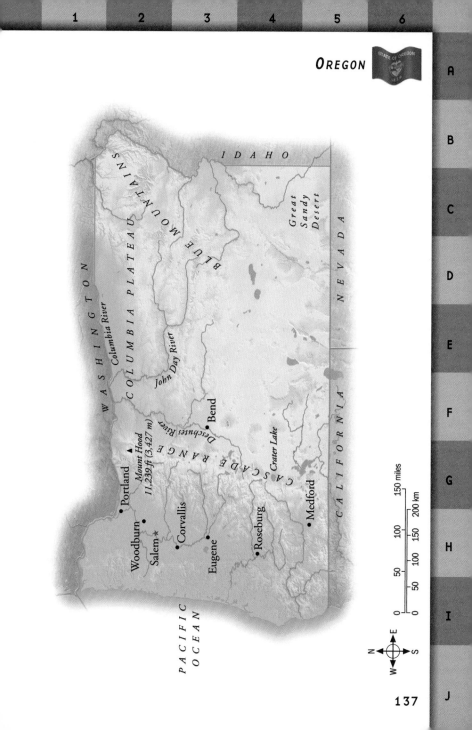

OREGON

Washington

Washington

Washington's ragged coastline includes the mountainous Olympic Peninsula, a cool northern rain forest with mosses and ferns. The state's biggest city is the seaport of Seattle, on Puget Sound. Seattle's modern skyscrapers look out to sea or inland toward distant Mount Rainier (14,409 ft/4,392 m), in the northern Cascade Range. In the eastern part of the state are river valleys, forests, and rugged highlands. The state's forests provide timber, and its farms produce vegetables, grapes, and fine-quality apples. Many of Washington's rivers are used to generate hydroelectric power for cities and industries, such as aircraft manufacturing, computing, and electronics.

▶ *The Space Needle (center), opened in 1962, rises 605 ft (184 m) above the city of Seattle.*

DISCOVER MORE
Washington's Olympic Peninsula is about as wet as it gets. It has the highest rainfall in the continental U.S.A., receiving about 144 in (3,658 mm) each year.

SEARCH AND FIND

★Olympia	.H4	Spokane	.C3
Bellingham	.G2	Tacoma	.G3
Bremerton	.G3	Vancouver	.G5
Kenniwick	.D4	Walla Walla	.C4
Seattle	.G3		

WASHINGTON FACTS

Statehood Date (Order)	Area sq mi (sq km)	Population	Flower • Tree • Bird
November 11, 1889 (42ND)	68,139 (176,479)	6,287,759	Coast rhododendron • Western hemlock • Willow goldfinch

WASHINGTON

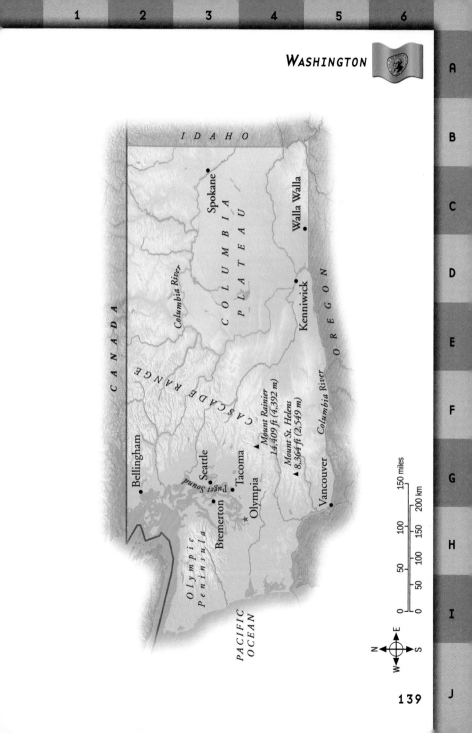

I D A H O

Spokane

Walla Walla

C O L U M B I A   P L A T E A U

Columbia River

Kenniwick

C A N A D A

C A S C A D E   R A N G E

O R E G O N

Mount Rainier
14,409 ft (4,392 m) ▲

Mount St. Helens
8,364 ft (2,549 m) ▲

Columbia River

Bellingham

Seattle

Tacoma

Olympia ★

Bremerton

Puget Sound

Vancouver

O l y m p i c   P e n i n s u l a

PACIFIC
OCEAN

150 miles

200 km

100

150

50

100

50

100

0

0

N
E
S
W

A B C D E F G H I J

Pacific States

Alaska

United States

Hawaii

Alaska, the largest state in the U.S.A., occupies the far northwest of the North America. It is bordered by Canada and lies just 56 mi (90 km) away from Russia. Alaska is a wilderness of frozen tundra, mountains, glaciers, and foggy coastlines. Industries include fisheries and oil.

The state of Hawaii is made up of a string of volcanic islands that are situated in the middle of the Pacific Ocean. These enjoy a lush tropical climate that attracts tourists and enables crops such as pineapples and sugarcane to be grown.

▲ Fountaining lava spews from the top of a volcano in Hawaii's Volcanoes National Park.

DISCOVER MORE

In parts of northern Alaska, the Earth's curve means that for 2 months in winter the Sun never rises and it is dark all day. Then for 85 days in summer the Sun never sets.

SEARCH AND FIND

Alaska	Hawaii
Juneau. D6	Honolulu. G3

REGION FACTS

	Highest elevation	Lowest elevation	State nickname	Major river(s)
Alaska	Mount McKinley 20,320 ft (6,194 m)	Sea level	The Last Frontier or Land of the Midnight Sun	Kuskokwim, Yukon, Colville
Hawaii	Mauna Kea 13,796 ft (4,205 m)	Sea level	Aloha State	Wailuku, Anahula, Opaeula

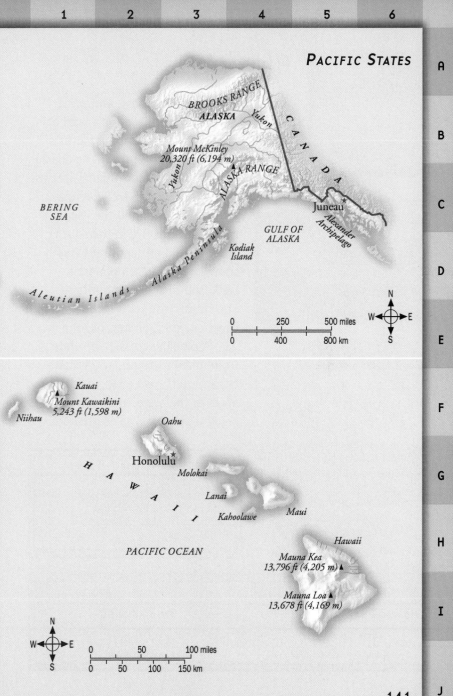

PACIFIC STATES

1 2 3 4 5 6

A B C D E F G H I J

BROOKS RANGE

ALASKA

Yukon

C A N A D A

Mount McKinley
20,320 ft (6,194 m) ▲

ALASKA RANGE

Yukon

BERING
SEA

Juneau ★

Alexander
Archipelago

GULF OF
ALASKA

Kodiak
Island

Aleutian Islands   Alaska Peninsula

| 0 | 250 | 500 miles |
| 0 | 400 | 800 km |

N
W ◆ E
S

Kauai
Mount Kawaikini
5,243 ft (1,598 m) ▲

Niihau

Oahu

Honolulu ★

Molokai

H
A
W
A
I
I

Lanai

Kahoolawe

Maui

PACIFIC OCEAN

Hawaii

Mauna Kea
13,796 ft (4,205 m) ▲

Mauna Loa ▲
13,678 ft (4,169 m)

N
W ◆ E
S

| 0 | 50 | 100 miles |
| 0 | 50 | 100 | 150 km |

Alaska

Alaska

Alaska is the largest, coldest, and most northerly state in the U.S.A. It is a land of remote wilderness, icy mountains, forests, glaciers, and foggy islands. An Arctic coastal plain is made up of the deep-frozen, treeless soil called *tundra*. Arctic peoples include the Inuit and the Aleuts. Most Alaskans live in the south, 4 out of 10 in Anchorage. This sprawling city is set against a backdrop of snowy mountains. The state's resources include fisheries, gold, timber, oil, and gas. A pipeline crosses the state from north to south. Tourists are beginning to visit even remote areas of the state, and many enjoy watching whales offshore.

▲ *A glacier at Prince William Sound, on the southern coast of Alaska. The Sound contains numerous small islands.*

DISCOVER MORE
Mount McKinley, in the Denali National Park, has its head in the clouds. Its icy peak stands 20,320 ft (6,194 m) above sea level, the tallest mountain in all of North America.

SEARCH AND FIND

★Juneau	C4	Ketchikan	B4
Anchorage	D3	Nome	F2
Barrow	E1	Sitka	C4
Fairbanks	D3		

ALASKA FACTS

Statehood Date (Order)	Area sq mi (sq km)	Population	Flower • Tree • Bird
January 3, 1959 (49TH)	591,004 (1,530,700)	663,661	Forget-me-not • Sitka spruce • Willow ptarmigan

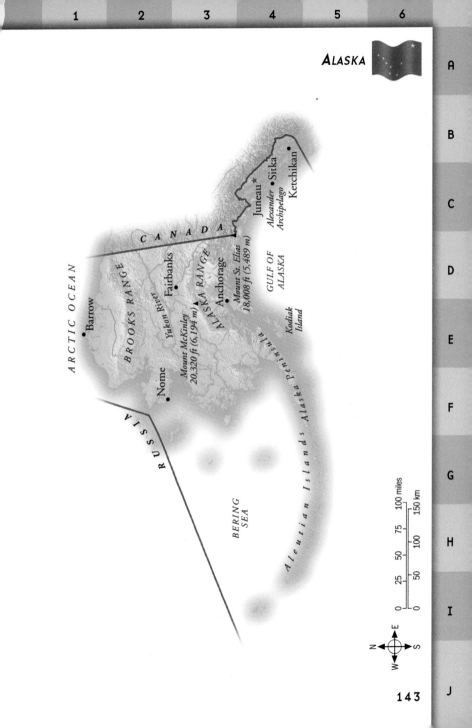

ALASKA

1 2 3 4 5 6

A
B
C
D
E
F
G
H
I
J

ARCTIC OCEAN

Barrow

BROOKS RANGE

CANADA

Fairbanks

Yukon River

Nome

Mount McKinley
20,320 ft (6,194 m)

ALASKA RANGE

Anchorage

Mount St. Elias
18,008 ft (5,489 m)

GULF OF
ALASKA

Juneau ★

Alexander • Sitka
Archipelago

Ketchikan

Kodiak
Island

RUSSIA

BERING
SEA

Aleutian Islands Alaska Peninsula

100 miles
150 km
75
100
50
50
25
0
0

N E
W S

Hawaii

Hawaii

The state of Hawaii is made up of a chain of lush, tropical islands that lie about 2,500 mi (4,023 km) from the U.S. mainland. They are in fact the peaks of underwater volcanoes, rising from the floor of the Pacific Ocean. The four chief islands are called Hawaii, Maui, Oahu, and Kauai. Eruptions of molten lava are still forming new rocks, as they cool and harden. Many mainland Americans settle here and the islands are popular with tourists. Fertile valleys produce pineapples and sugarcane. The chief city and seaport is Honolulu, which is backed by high volcanic cliffs on the southern coast of Oahu.

▲ *Hawaii's beautiful beaches, lying along the Pacific Ocean, are bordered by palm trees.*

DISCOVER MORE

Surfing was invented by the Hawaiian islanders. It was here that surfers and surfboards were first described in detail in 1779 by a visiting British naval officer.

SEARCH AND FIND

★Honolulu	.F3	Kailua	.F2
Hilo	.C4	Kaneohe	.F2
Kahului	.D3	Waipahu	.F2

HAWAII FACTS

Statehood Date (Order)	Area sq mi (sq km)	Population	Flower • Tree • Bird
August 21, 1959 (50TH)	6,471 (16,759)	1,275,194	Red hibiscus • Kukui (candlenut) • Nene (Hawaiian goose)

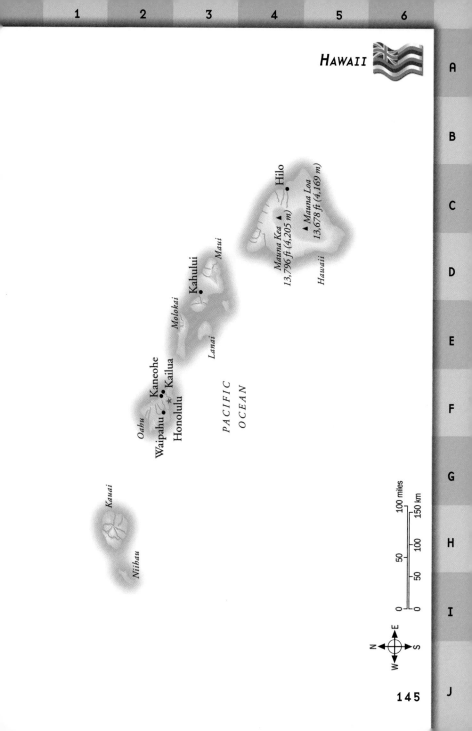

Hilo

Mauna Kea ▲
13,796 ft (4,205 m)

▲ Mauna Loa
13,678 ft (4,169 m)

Maui

Kahului

Molokai

Lanai

Hawaii

Kaneohe
Kailua
Oahu
★
Waipahu
Honolulu

PACIFIC
OCEAN

Kauai

Niihau

100 miles

150 km

100

50

50

0

0

N
W — E
S

U.S. Territories

There are 14 islands, or groups of islands, that are territories of the United States. This means they are administered by the U.S. government. Only 5 of these territories are permanently inhabited: American Samoa, Guam, Puerto Rico, the U.S. Virgin Islands, and the Northern Mariana Islands. Wake Island, in the South Pacific, is used as an airstrip by the U.S. military. The remainder of the territories are tiny wildlife refuges made up of low-lying sandy coral islands.

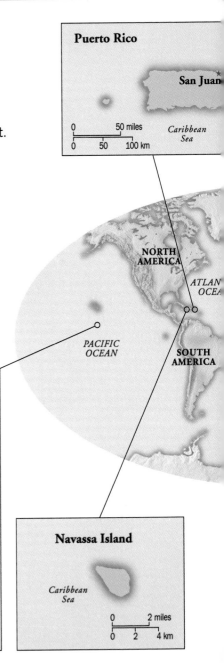

Puerto Rico

San Juan

0   50 miles
0   50   100 km

Caribbean
Sea

NORTH
AMERICA

ATLANTIC
OCEAN

PACIFIC
OCEAN

SOUTH
AMERICA

0   500 miles
0   1000 km

Midway
Islands

Johnston
Atoll

Kingman
Reef

Howland
Island

Palmyra
Atoll

Baker
Island

Jarvis
Island

Navassa Island

Caribbean
Sea

0   2 miles
0   2   4 km

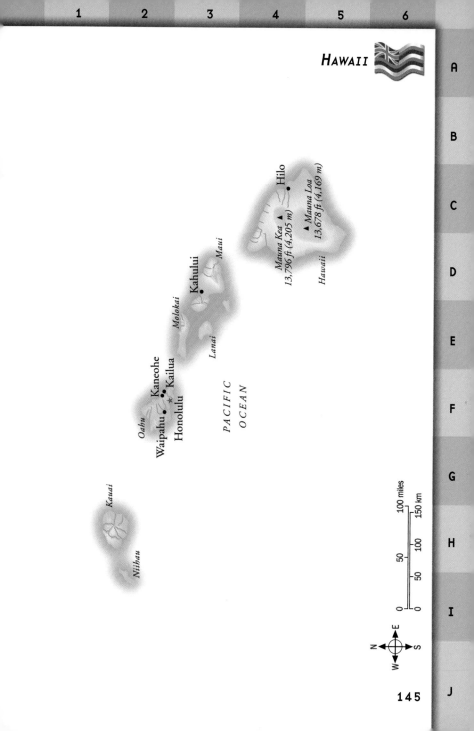

HAWAII

A

B

Hilo

Mauna Kea ▲
13,796 ft (4,205 m)

▲ Mauna Loa
13,678 ft (4,169 m)

C

Hawaii

D

Kahului

Maui

Molokai

Lanai

E

PACIFIC
OCEAN

F

Kaneohe
Kailua
Oahu
Waipahu ★
Honolulu

G

Kauai

100 miles

150 km

100

H

Niihau

50   50

I

0   0

N
E
S
W

J

U.S. Territories

There are 14 islands, or groups of islands, that are territories of the United States. This means they are administered by the U.S. government. Only 5 of these territories are permanently inhabited: American Samoa, Guam, Puerto Rico, the U.S. Virgin Islands, and the Northern Mariana Islands. Wake Island, in the South Pacific, is used as an airstrip by the U.S. military. The remainder of the territories are tiny wildlife refuges made up of low-lying sandy coral islands.

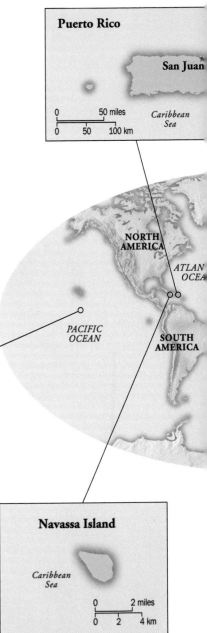

Puerto Rico

San Juan

0   50 miles

0   50   100 km

Caribbean Sea

NORTH AMERICA

ATLANTIC OCEAN

PACIFIC OCEAN

SOUTH AMERICA

0   500 miles

0   1000 km

Midway Islands

Johnston Atoll

Kingman Reef

Howland Island

Palmyra Atoll

Baker Island

Jarvis Island

Navassa Island

Caribbean Sea

0   2 miles

0   2   4 km

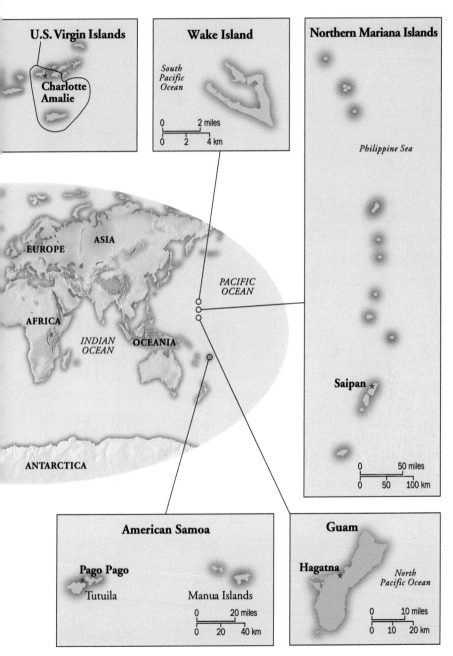

U.S. Virgin Islands

Charlotte
Amalie

Wake Island

South
Pacific
Ocean

0   2 miles
0   2   4 km

Northern Mariana Islands

Philippine Sea

ASIA

EUROPE

*PACIFIC
OCEAN*

AFRICA

*INDIAN
OCEAN*   OCEANIA

ANTARCTICA

Saipan

0   50 miles
0   50   100 km

American Samoa

Pago Pago

Tutuila   Manua Islands

0   20 miles
0   20   40 km

Guam

Hagatna   North
Pacific Ocean

0   10 miles
0   10   20 km

Puerto Rico

Puerto Rico is a small territory found in the Greater Antilles island chain, which fringes the Caribbean Sea. It is not a state, but a self-governing "Commonwealth" of the U.S.A. The climate is tropical and crops grown for export include sugarcane, rice, and pineapples. A forested mountain range, the Cordillera Central, runs parallel to the southern coast. The capital, San Juan, is on the northern coast. The most widely spoken language is the local form of Spanish.

▶ *Columbus Square in San Juan was named in 1893 on the 400th anniversary of Christopher Columbus' discovery of Puerto Rico.*

DISCOVER MORE
The world's largest single-unit radio telescope at the Arecibo Observatory has been used to send signals to parts of the galaxy that may be home to other forms of life.

SEARCH AND FIND

★San Juan	E3	Caguas	E3
Aguadilla	G3	Mayagüez	G3
Arecibo	F3	Ponce	F4
Bayamon	E3		

PUERTO RICO FACTS

Statehood Date (Order)	Area sq mi (sq km)	Population	Flower • Tree • Bird
none	3,515 (9,104)	3,858,806	Puerto Rican hibiscus • Silk-cotton tree • Stripe-headed tanager

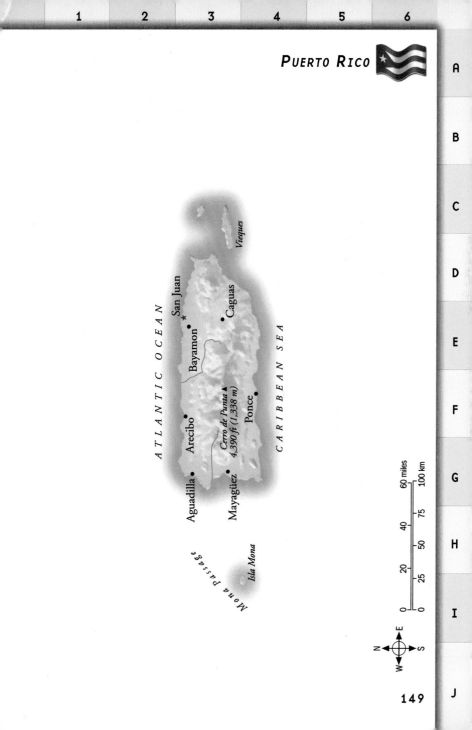

A

B

C

Vieques

D

ATLANTIC OCEAN

San Juan

Caguas

Bayamon

E

CARIBBEAN SEA

Cerro de Punta ▲
4,390 ft (1,338 m)

Ponce

F

Arecibo

G

Aguadilla

Mayagüez

60 miles
100 km

40
75

H

Mona Passage

Isla Mona

20
50
25

I

0
0

E
N ✦ S
W

J

U.S. Territorial Expansion

In 1783, at the end of the American Revolution, the territory of the United States was bordered to the north by Canada, to the west by the Mississippi River, to the south by the Spanish colonies of East and West Florida, and to the east by the Atlantic Ocean. Over the following 115 years, the U.S.A. acquired further land in a variety of ways, including buying it from other states, negotiating it through treaties, and winning it in wars. This map shows when the various parts of the present-day United States were acquired.

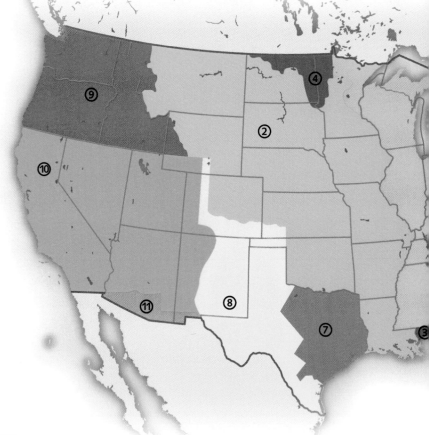

Key

① United States (1783)
② Louisiana Purchase (1803)
③ West Florida Annexation
   (1810–1813)
④ Claimed by Britain until 1818
⑤ Florida Cession (1819)
⑥ Claimed by Britain until 1842
⑦ Texas Annexation (1845)
⑧ Claimed by Spain until 1848
⑨ Claimed by Britain until 1846
⑩ Mexican Cession (1848)
⑪ Gadsen Purchase (1853)
⑫ Alaska Purchase (1867)
⑬ Hawaiian Annexation (1898)

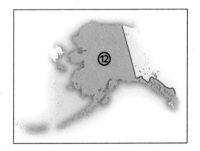

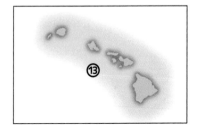

Flags of the U.S.A.

Every state in the U.S.A. has its own flag, shown here. The country also has a national flag, and flags for its dependencies, also shown.

National Flag

The United States flag is commonly known as "the Stars and Stripes" or "Old Glory." It consists of 13 horizontal stripes, 7 of which are red, and 6 white. These stripes symbolize the 13 original colonies. The 50 small white, five-pointed stars represent America's 50 states.

State Flags

Alabama	Alaska	Arizona	Arkansas	California
Colorado	Connecticut	Delaware	District of Columbia*	Florida
Georgia	Hawaii	Idaho	Illinois	Indiana
Iowa	Kansas	Kentucky	Louisiana	Maine
Maryland	Massachusetts	Michigan	Minnesota	Mississippi

Missouri · Montana · Nebraska · Nevada · New Hampshire

New Jersey · New Mexico · New York · North Carolina · North Dakota

Ohio · Oklahoma · Oregon · Pennsylvania · Rhode Island

South Carolina · South Dakota · Tennessee · Texas · Utah

Vermont · Virginia · Washington · West Virginia · Wisconsin

Wyoming

* District of Columbia is a federal district, not a state.

U.S. Territory Flags

Of the 14 territories of the United States (see pages 146–49), the 5 shown here have their own flags. The remaining territories take the Stars and Stripes as their flag. These territories are Baker Island, Howland Island, Jarvis Island, Johnston Atoll, Kingman Reef, Midway Islands, Palmyra Atoll, Navassa Island, and Wake Island.

American Samoa

Guam

Northern Marianas

Puerto Rico

U.S. Virgin Islands

Glossary

altitude the height of land above sea level.

archipelago a group of islands that are close together.

basin 1. a bowl-shaped area of land that is lower than the surrounding area. 2. an area of land through which a river flows.

bay an inlet in the coastline of an ocean or lake, normally eroded by the waves.

bluff a steep cliff.

border 1. the edge of an area of land or vegetation. 2. the area between two countries. 3. a boundary.

boundary a nonphysical line that separates one country or area of land from another.

butte a steep-sided rock that stands on its own and rises sharply above the land around it.

canal a human-made waterway used for transportation or irrigation.

canyon a deep valley, with steep sides, which often has a river flowing through it.

cape a region of land that projects from the coastline into an ocean.

capital a location officially designated as the chief city of a nation, state, province, or territory; often the center of government.

channel a navigable stretch of water between two areas of land.

cinder cone a cone-shaped volcano that is made from layers of dust and tiny pieces of rock.

climate the pattern of weather conditions normally recorded in any one place or region.

coast land bordering an ocean.

compass rose the points of the compass, as displayed on a map.

continent a landmass or part of a landmass, making up one of the 7 major geographical divisions of the world.

coral hard rock that is made from the shells and skeletons of tiny sea creatures.

crag a steep, rough rock formation.

crater 1. a large opening or depression at the top of a volcano. 2. a hollow in the land caused when a meteor crashes to Earth.

crust the thin layer of rock that covers Earth's surface.

current the movement of water over long distances in seas, oceans, and rivers.

delta an area in which a river splits into several separate waterways before entering the sea or lake. It is normally created by deposits of mud or sand. The name comes from the triangular shape of such a region, which looks like the Greek letter delta (Δ).

desert an area of land that has very little or no rain.

divide a ridge or line of crests separating two drainage areas.

earthquake a shaking of the ground that happens when sections of Earth's crust move.

elevation the height above sea or ground level.

equator an imaginary horizontal line around the middle of the globe, halfway between the North Pole and the South Pole.

estuary a river mouth, where freshwater meets and mixes with the salt water from an ocean or sea.

ethnic group a group of people sharing common descent, language, or culture.

fault line a fracture in Earth's surface along which sections of crust are forced together, or slide past one another, sometimes causing earthquakes.

fjord a long, deep-sea inlet formed by glaciers in prehistoric times.

floodplain the flat land on either side of a river that is covered by water when the river floods.

forest any large area of dense woodland.

geyser jets of hot water and steam that gush up into the air. They are formed when rainwater seeps into the rocks and is heated by volcanic forces deep underground.

glacier a large body of ice that moves slowly along a valley or down a mountain.

gorge a narrow valley, with steep rocky sides, through which a river runs.

Greenwich Mean Time (GMT) the mean solar time of the Greenwich Meridian, used throughout the world as the basis of standard time.

Greenwich Meridian the line of longitude (0°) from which distances to the east or west are measured. It passes through Greenwich, England. Also called the prime meridian.

grid a crisscross network of lines used to locate places on a map.

gulf an area of seawater that reaches into the land. A gulf is usually wide, with a narrow opening into the sea.

harbor a natural or human-made sea inlet that protects boats at their moorings.

hemisphere the globe divided into two halves, either north and south or east and west.

hill land that rises from the ground around it but is not as high as a mountain.

iceberg a large chunk of ice that floats in seas and oceans. Most of the iceberg lies hidden beneath the water's surface.

inlet a narrow stretch of water that cuts into the land from a sea or a river.

island an area of land completely surrounded by water.

Glossary

isthmus a narrow stretch of land connecting two larger bodies of land.

lagoon a body of salt water that is separated from the sea by a strip of land.

lake a body of water that is surrounded by land.

landlocked surrounded by land on all sides, with no coastline.

latitude the location of a place north or south of the equator, that is measured in degrees. Measurements are determined using horizontal lines that circle the globe, parallel to the equator.

lava the hot liquid rock that pours out of a volcano during an eruption.

levee a wall that is built along a riverbank to stop the river from flooding.

longitude the location of a place located east or west of the Greenwich meridian, measured in degrees. Measurements are determined using imaginary vertical lines, called meridians, which run from the North Pole to the South Pole.

marsh an area of very wet land that is usually low-lying.

mesa a rocky hill or mountain with a flat top and steep sides.

mineral a natural substance, such as gold and copper, that is formed deep inside the earth.

monsoon a strong wind that brings heavy rains in the summer months in the Indian Ocean and southern Asia.

moor an area of rough, open, high ground, often boggy.

mountain a very high area of land.

mountain pass a route from one side of a mountain range to the other.

mountain range a chain of high peaks and ridges.

mountain system a chain of mountain ranges, or ranges sharing the same geological origins.

oasis a place in the desert where there is water and some vegetation.

ocean a very large area of salt water on Earth's surface.

paddy a flooded field in which rice plants are grown.

pampas South American grasslands.

peak the highest point of a mountain.

peninsula a strip of land that sticks out into the sea and is almost completely surrounded by water.

pinnacle a column of rock, eroded to a slender point.

plain a large area of flat land.

plateau an area of high ground that is usually very flat.

population the people or the number of individuals living in a given place.

prairie the flat, grass-covered lands of North America.

rain forest forests with dense, evergreen vegetation fed by high rainfall. The term normally refers to tropical forests, but can also mean similar forests in temperate regions.

reef a platform of rocks or coral just below the surface of the sea.

ridge a thin stretch of high ground. ·

rift valley a long valley created by movement along a fault line in Earth's crust.

river a moderate-to-large body of water draining off the land and normally flowing between banks toward other rivers or the ocean.

salt flat a large area of flat land that is covered with crystals of salt.

sand dune a hill of sand that is formed by the wind.

savanna a wide grassy plain with a few scattered trees.

scale a distance on a map shown in proportion to the real distance.

scrub an area of land that is thickly covered with low-growing trees and shrubs.

sea a body of salt water, making up an arm or region of an ocean.

solar energy energy that is produced using the Sun's rays.

steppe a wide area of flat grass-covered land in eastern Europe and central Asia.

strait a narrow stretch of water connecting two larger bodies of water.

subtropics the regions bordering the tropics.

swamp an area of wet, muddy land.

territory 1. an area of land that does not have the status of an independent nation. 2. a province or region within a nation.

time zone a large area where every place has the same time. The world is divided into 24 different time zones. The time in each zone is one hour behind or in front of the time in the neighboring zones.

tributary a stream or river that flows into another one during its journey to the ocean.

tropics the warm regions between the Tropic of Cancer and the Tropic of Capricorn near the equator.

tundra cold, bare land where the soil is frozen for long periods of each year. Only small, low-lying plants can grow on the tundra.

valley a low-lying area that is eroded from the land by a river or glacier between two hills or mountains.

veldt the open, grassy plains of southern Africa.

volcano a weak point in Earth's crust, where molten lava bursts through the surface. Lava eruptions may build up to form a mountain.

wetland an area of wet ground.

Index

Numbers in **bold** type refer to main entries. Numbers in *italics* refer to illustrations.

Index

D

Index

Index

M

Index

Index

Index

S

Index

Acknowledgments

**The publishers would like to thank the following
sources for the use of their photographs:**

15 (BR) Scott Olson/Getty Images; 16 (B) Bill Pugliano/Getty Images; 17 (T) Mario
Tama/Getty Images; 26 Rudi von Briel/Photolibrary; 30 Glenn LeBlanc/Photolibrary;
32 Bill Bachmann/Photolibrary; 34 Robert Francis/Photolibrary; 36 Wolfgang
Kaehler/Corbis; 38 Gail Dohrmann/Photolibrary; 42 Bo Zaunders/Corbis; 46 Linda Reeves
/Photolibrary; 48 Barry Winiker/Photolibrary; 50 Raeanne Rubenstein/Photolibrary;
54 Jim Schwabel/Photolibrary; 56 Charlie Borland/Photolibrary; 58 Stan Osolinski/
Photolibrary; 62 Wendell Metzen/Photolibrary; 64 Wendell Metzen/Photolibrary;
68 Willard Clay/Photolibrary; 70 Jim Schwabel/Photolibrary; 72 Chad Ehlers/Photolibrary;
74 Barry Winiker/Photolibrary; 76 Cameron Davidson /Photolibrary; 78 Robert Finken/
Photolibrary; 84 Walter Bibikow/Photolibrary; 86 Gene Moore/Photolibrary; 88 GMBH
IFA–BILDERTEAM/Photolibrary; 92 Bill Bachmann/Photolibrary; 96 Martin Sundberg
Photography/Photolibrary; 98 Erwin Bud Nielsen/Photolibrary; 100 Stephen Saks/
Photolibrary; 102 Bill Bachmann/Photolibrary; 108 Willard Clay/Photolibrary; 110 Resnick
Seth/Photolibrary; 112 James Schwabel/Photolibrary; 114 Jeff Friedman/Photolibrary;
116 Lynn Stone/Photolibrary; 122 Walter Bibikow/Photolibrary; 124 Rob Blakers/
Photolibrary; 140 David Reggie/Photolibrary; 148 Wendell Metzen/Photolibrary

All other photographs are from MKP Archives (Corel, PhotoDisc).

The publisher has made every effort to contact all copyright holders
but apologizes if any source remains unacknowledged.

On-the-go reference books for your on-the-go life!

Collect them all!

❏ 0-439-62039-2	Scholastic Pocket Dictionary	$7.95
❏ 0-439-62037-6	Scholastic Pocket Thesaurus	$6.95
❏ 0-439-68193-6	Scholastic Pocket World Atlas	$8.95

Available wherever you buy books, or use this order form.